THE BOOK OF
BOND STREET
OLD AND NEW

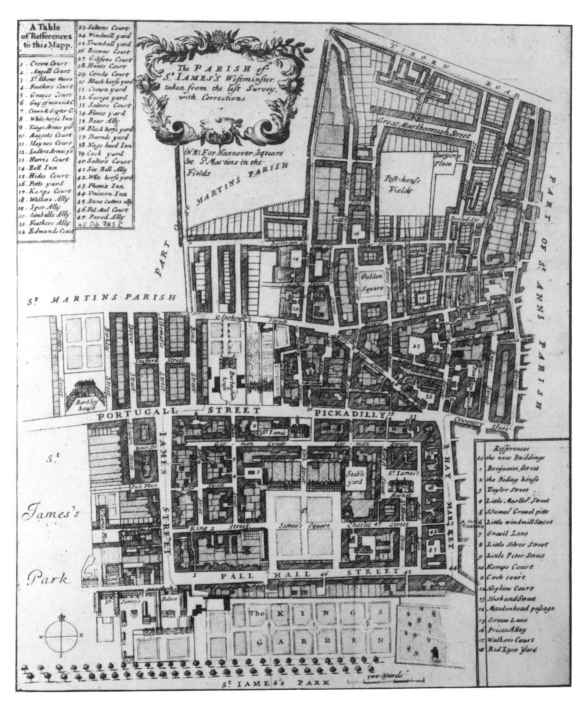

Map of the Parish of St James's, Westminster, 1720, showing Bond Street

THE BOOK OF
BOND STREET
OLD AND NEW

By

JEAN DESEBROCK

B. Litt. (Oxon.)

Partly based on material
compiled by

H. B. WHEATLEY, F.S.A.

TALLIS PRESS

© Tallis Press Ltd 1978

Made and printed
in Great Britain
by Anchor Press Ltd
Tiptree and London
for
TALLIS PRESS LTD
115 Old Street London EC1

CONTENTS

LIST OF ILLUSTRATIONS

Chapter One

BEGINNINGS

*   *   *

Internationally renowned today, as for many years past, for its luxury clothes, its jewellers and other fine shops of exquisite taste, and of course its picture galleries, Bond Street has, for nearly three centuries, been a foremost home of fashion. Always one of the chief thoroughfares of the West End, it is today, as it was from the start, the resort of worth and worldly aspirations, with a history which has made it one of the best known streets in the world. From the time when its first fine houses arose, Bond Street became and remained one of the most fashionable and desirable addresses in London; and to this day, while its character has gradually become more purely commercial, it has kept and increased its attractions for shoppers of taste.

The renown of Bond Street is well deserved, and those who pass along its crowded pavements and road today must still feel that they are moving in the very heart of London's fashionable life. In spite of rebuildings, the long lines of properties, an untidily irregular assortment, tell of the original formation; moments of the street's distinguished history are still to be found wherever one looks.

Old Bond Street was laid out in 1686, New Bond Street, as far as Clifford Street, soon after 1700, and the extension to Oxford Street began in 1721.

Before dealing with the history of the street itself, it will be well to give a glance back at the condition of the site, and try to obtain a general idea of the state of the district when it was first built.

Back in the early seventeenth century, before the fine streets of Mayfair were dreamt of, the quiet countryside on which they were to arise was an area of undulating farmlands populated only by the inhabitants of a couple of farmhouses and a single windmill. The area did not begin to develop until much later in that century, after the Restoration of the Monarchy, and many Mayfair streets were to bear the names of followers of Charles II. Among these was Bond Street itself, named after Sir Thomas Bond, and also Burlington Street, Albemarle Street, Dover Street, Berkeley and Stratton Streets, and Hamilton Place.

When the followers of the exiled Charles II returned to London they found that the residential parts of town had undergone considerable changes in their absence. Pall Mall, which they left an open space, in which the game of pell mell was played, was partially built upon, and play was transferred to St James's Park when the present Mall was prepared for that purpose.

At this time the name Piccadilly was applied only to the eastern end of the present-day street, the area near the Haymarket, running no further west than the foot of Sackville Street. The remainder of the thoroughfare was a country road leading to Kensington and to Reading and Bath. After the Restoration, the road between Sackville and Albemarle Streets – and later as far as Hyde Park – was called Portugal Street as a compliment to Catherine of Braganza, Queen of Charles II (just as Pall Mall was for a time known as Catherine Street), though at this period it was just an open lane leading to the Great Western Road, itself a rough track frequented by highwaymen. The Queen was not a favourite with her people, however, and gradually the name Piccadilly displaced her memory.

In the late seventeenth century there was still, to the north of St James's Palace, a wide area of open countryside, the neighbourhood of Bond Street being unpopulated and swampy. Puget, Sieur de la Serre, the French historiographer who accompanied Queen Marie de

Medicis on her visit to her daughter, Henrietta Maria, in 1638, had written of St James's Palace: "Its great gate has a long street in front, reaching almost out of sight, seemingly joining to the fields." This was still true at the Restoration, though those fields were soon to be covered with houses. By the beginning of the reign of George IV the area between Piccadilly and Oxford Street was to become the headquarters of the fashionable world.

Lord Macaulay describes this district in the last year of the reign of Charles II (1685) as follows: "He who then rambled to what is now the gayest and most crowded part of Regent Street, found himself in a solitude, and was sometimes so fortunate as to have a shot at a woodcock. On the north the Oxford road ran between hedges. Three or four hundred yards to the south were the garden-walls of a few great houses, which were considered as quite out of town. On the west was a meadow, renowned for a spring, from which, long afterwards, Conduit Street was named. On the east (near where now stands Golden Square) was a field not to be passed without a shudder by any Londoner of that age. There, as in a place far from the haunts of men, had been dug, twenty years before, when the great plague was raging, a pit into which the dead-carts had nightly shot corpses by scores. It was popularly believed that the earth was deeply tainted with infection, and could not be disturbed without imminent risk till two generations had passed without any return of the pestilence, and till the ghastly spot had long been surrounded by buildings. It may be added, that the 'pest-field' may still be seen marked in maps of London as late as the end of the reign of George I."

Along what is now Piccadilly there were built, when this westernmost edge of London was still covered by fields, and Piccadilly (or Portugal Street) was little more than a country lane, some fine seventeenth-century mansions of the nobility, referred to in the above passage. The first to be built was Goring House, on what is now Arlington Street. Almost opposite it arose the most notable of the mansions, Clarendon

3

Clarendon House c.1668, which stood on the site of Old Bond Street

House, on the north side of Piccadilly, on the site later to be occupied by Old Bond Street, Albemarle Street, Dover Street and Stafford Street. Built by Edward Hyde, the great Lord Chancellor Clarendon, between 1664 and 1667, it was from the beginning an unmitigated disaster. Within three years of its building it had become a sad monument to fallen greatness; within twenty it was gone.

Some thirty acres of land to the north of Piccadilly had been granted to Clarendon by Charles II. The grant by Letters Patent, dated June 13th, 1664, contains particulars of this land, although it is difficult to fix the boundaries in modern terms. It seems to have extended eastwards as far as Swallow Street (later largely absorbed by Regent Street), the western extent being less clear. On March 7th, 1666, Clarendon's lands were further augmented: a lease of the Conduit Mead (on which was to arise New Bond Street, Conduit Street, Brook Street and other streets) was granted to Clarendon by the City of London for ninety-nine years at a nominal rent of £8 a year.

Two other noblemen followed Clarendon's lead and built fine houses along Piccadilly, further improving the social status of this rising neighbourhood. It seems that they acquired at least some of their land from him. Lord Burlington built his mansion to the east, and Lord Berkeley of Stratton his to the west of Clarendon House. Though also splendid, neither of these mansions was as sumptuous as Clarendon House, and the progress of neither was so jealously watched.

The corruption and licentiousness of Charles II's newly established court was soon being criticised, not least by Edward Hyde, Lord Clarendon. In the seventeenth century the office of Lord Chancellor (or Prime Minister) was one of immense power and wealth, and it was not surprising that Clarendon had his enemies who were keen to bring him down, one of the most vicious being Barbara Castlemaine, a mistress of the King, and others, who wielded immense power at court, having a talent for inducing Charles to make the appointments she wished and by which she was able to make large sums of money – a

5

practice which would, more usually, belong to the Chancellor. Clarendon, somewhat old and dour for the gaudy butterfly collection at court, did not have the gift of winning friends and popularity, though the King, it was recognised, depended upon him "for his policy and his service".

It has been suggested that the building of Clarendon House (which eventually cost Clarendon £50,000, which was £30,000 over the original estimate) was the act of a man whose head was turned by high position. In 1664 he was at the apex of his power, Lord Chancellor of England and still capable of dominating his inexperienced King, though Charles was already growing tired of his overbearing grip. However, Clarendon had been granted money together with his land, and the originally projected cost of £20,000 for the house would not have been beyond his means. Gilbert Burnet wrote: "He had intended a good, ordinary house, but, not understanding these matters himself, he put the managing of that into the hands of others, who ran him into a vast charge, of about £50,000, three times as much as he had designed to lay out upon it."

The house was commenced immediately in 1664 on a site directly opposite St James's Street: it had a fine view looking down on St James's Palace (a fact resented by Clarendon's enemies who suggested that he had placed himself above the King). The Earl (in another step which was to win criticism) bought the stones which had, before the Civil War, been prepared for the renovation of old St Paul's Cathedral. As this was destroyed in the Great Fire, the stones were no longer of use for this purpose and Clarendon acquired them for the building of his house, on which three hundred men were, in a time of serious unemployment, usefully engaged.

Clarendon House was, by all accounts, magnificent. Its grounds, in terms of the streets which were later to arise on their site, stretched from Dover Street in the west to Old Bond Street in the east, and up to Grafton Street in the north. The enormous square mansion consisted of a centre section with two wings, forming three sides of a quadrangle. It was a heavy, high-roofed house, standing a little back from the street and approached by a short, wide flight of steps; it had square-headed windows, including a row of attic windows which pierced the roof. There were two principal floors and an attic storey surmounted by a balustrade, with a small domed tower in the centre. Along Piccadilly there ran a low wall with a line of trees and a handsome gateway.

Clarendon House was designed by a "friend and fellow traveller" of John Evelyn, Sir Roger Pratt, and the diarist was perhaps prejudiced in its favour on that account, for he speaks very highly of the house in a letter to Lord Cornbury, Clarendon's eldest son, declaring that "I have never seen a nobler pile . . . It is, without hyperboles, the best contrived, the most useful, graceful, and magnificent house in England . . . here is state and use, solidity and beauty most symmetrically combined together: seriously there is nothing abroad pleases me better; nothing at home approaches it." He goes on to express the wish: "May that great and illustrious person whose large and ample heart has honoured his country with so glorious a structure . . . live many long years to enjoy it" – but in fact the fine house had a very short history, and Clarendon himself was to fall even sooner.

At a later date Evelyn noticed defects in the architecture of the house, but still considered it a noble palace, most gracefully placed. The elevation appeared somewhat commonplace, but the interior was well arranged, and described by Duke Cosmo III in 1669 as "commodious and sumptuous". Samuel Pepys, who visited it in April 1667, describes the house as "very noble", with "brave pictures of the ancient and present nobility, never saw better" – pictures which had been selected by Evelyn, who had also assisted in the planning of the gardens.

The building of this house proved a most ill-advised proceeding, of immense cost to Clarendon both in terms of money and unpopularity. His estate was greatly injured by the financial burden and his enemies took the opportunity of imbuing the populace with their own prejudices against him.

Because the house was built partly with stones designed for the repair of old St Paul's, Clarendon was said to have turned to a profane use what he had bought with a bribe. It is a curious coincidence that the same charge was made at the building of Somerset House, the difference being that the Duke of Somerset stole the stones, and Clarendon bought his.

The Plague and the Great Fire of 1666, the unsuccessful war with Holland and the failure of the Queen to produce an heir to the throne were all circumstances which combined to cause a widespread feeling of discontent among the inhabitants of London, which vented itself upon the Government of which Clarendon was the unfortunate head. The people, with jealous eyes on the progress of his mansion, were incensed against him for his reckless expenditure – and indeed the building of Clarendon House had been undertaken at a most unfortunate time.

It was scarcely just, of course, that Clarendon should have been blamed for the Dutch war (which he had consistently opposed) or for the lack of a royal heir. His daughter had secretly married James, Duke of York, the King's brother, and it was suggested that Clarendon had engineered the marriage of Charles to Catherine of Braganza, knowing that she was barren, so that his own daughter and son-in-law should succeed to the throne.

The populace had singled out Clarendon to bear the whole brunt of their rage and when news came that the Dutch had come up the Thames to Gravesend and destroyed English ships, the mob broke the windows of Clarendon House, cut down trees and painted a gibbet on the gate, with the following lines beneath it:

> Three sights to be seen,
> Dunkirk, Tangiers, and a barren Queen.

The house was nicknamed Dunkirk House, because Clarendon was unjustly accused of having built it with money received from France for negotiating the sale of Dunkirk to Louis XIV; Holland House, because he was said to have received a bribe from the Dutch; and Tangier Hall on account of popular dissatisfaction at the cost of keeping up the garrison of that lately acquired dependency.

Andrew Marvell echoed all the unjust charges against him in *Clarendon's House Warming*, and the following lines, quoted by Isaac Disraeli from a contemporary manuscript, are equally severe:

> Lo! his whole ambition already divides
> The sceptre between the Stuarts and Hydes.
> Behold, in the depth of our Plague and Wars,
> He built him a Palace outbraves the stars;
> Which house (*we* Dunkirk, *he* Clarendon names)
> Looks down with shame upon St James;
> But it is not his golden globe will save him,
> Being less than the Custom-house farmers gave him;
> His chapel for consecration calls,
> Whose sacrilege plundered the stones from Paul's.

The damage which the mob had caused to Clarendon House was repaired and work continued on it, for it was then not yet complete. Clarendon must have known by this time that his days in high office were almost at an end: his attention and all his care was now lavished on his mansion, which became all-absorbing. When he at last moved into the house, Clarendon was old and ill, crippled with gout and bearing all the sorrows of the land upon his shoulders.

Quarrelling finally with the King, who was incensed at his suggestion that Barbara Castlemaine was the source of the trouble between them, Clarendon was, in August 1668, deprived of the Great Seal. For the next three months he lived on in Clarendon House, "too proud of a good conscience. He knew his own innocence and had no kind of apprehension of being publicly charged with any crime." However, Charles had no more use for him: he had at last outgrown him, and he allowed his enemies to have him impeached for high treason: Clarendon had to fly the kingdom to escape imprisonment and possible execution. He was to die in Calais seven years later, in 1674, never having returned to England.

The day before his flight, Evelyn "found him in his garden at his new-built palace, sitting in his gout wheelchair, and seeing the gates setting up towards the north and the fields. He looked and spake very disconsolately. Next morning I heard he was gone."

It is a sad picture: if Clarendon fell short of being a great man, he was at least zealous and strenuous; he had shared his master's exile and seen the King's cause triumph, only himself to fall. When he was impeached for high treason he wrote humbly to Charles: "I do upon my knees beg your pardon for any over-bold or saucy expressions I have used to you . . . a natural disease in old servants who have received too much countenance." He declared himself innocent of any charges of corruption or accepting money to which he had not been entitled.

In a volume of rare London ballads and broadsides in the British Library is one entitled "A Hue and Cry after the Earl of Clarendon", dated 1667:

> From Dunkirk House there lately ran away
> A traitor whom you are desired to slay.
> You by these marks and signs may th' traitor know,
> He's troubled with the gout in feet below.
>
> This hopeful blade being conscious of his crimes,
> And smelling how the current of the times
> Ran cross, forsakes his palace and the town
> Like some presaging rat ere th' house fall down.

Clarendon, in his autobiography, admits the "weakness and vanity" he had exhibited in the erection of his house, and "the gust" of envy which it drew upon him, and attributes his fall more to the fact that he had built such a house than to any misdemeanour of which he was thought to have been guilty. Lord Rochester, Clarendon's second son, told Lord Dartmouth that when his father left England he ordered him to tell all his friends "that if they could excuse the vanity and folly of the great house, he would undertake to answer for all the rest of his actions himself."

After Clarendon's flight his elder son, Lord Cornbury, lived in Clarendon House for a short time. Here Evelyn visited him on December 20th, 1668: "I dined with my Lord Cornbury at Clarendon House, now bravely furnished, especially with the pictures of most of our ancient and modern wits, poets, philosophers, famous and learned Englishmen . . ." Soon after this the house was let to an old friend of Clarendon's, the Duke of Ormonde, who was living there in 1670 when a strange and wild incident occurred.

On the evening of December 6th the Duke, then almost sixty and limp with gout, had been feasting at the Guildhall in attendance on the Prince of Orange, then paying a state visit to England. On his way home in his carriage to Clarendon House in the middle of a wintry dark night he was attacked in St James's Street and nearly kidnapped and murdered by the infamous Irishman Colonel Blood. The varied escapades of this most melodramatic of villains were much chronicled at the time and were indeed stranger than fiction, as was his convenient name.

The six footmen who invariably attended the Duke were always made to walk three on each side of his coach (he would not allow their weight on it, having spikes to prevent their clambering up). Blood's ruffians waylaid the footmen and the Duke was dragged from his coach.

The extraordinary Colonel Blood was not content with simple murder: he had a personal vendetta against the great Duke of Ormonde. During the Civil War Thomas Blood, who had first supported the Royalists, changed to the winning side and, as a result of services rendered, received, on the establishment of the Commonwealth, some fine English Crown lands greatly supplementing his own poor assets in Ireland. At the Restoration, however, these lands reverted to the Crown. A grievance was born. Returning to Ireland, where the Duke of Ormonde was then Lord Lieutenant and the man responsible, Blood attempted to capture Dublin Castle, aspiring to string the Duke up on a gibbet. The inept plan was neither successful nor disastrous: Blood made his escape; and when the Duke of Ormonde established himself in London, Blood was still on his tail.

Ormonde's attackers mounted him on horseback, buckling him to a sturdy one of their number and hurried him away past Berkeley House on the road to Tyburn, Blood having ridden ahead, anxious to tie a rope to the gallows in readiness.

Ormonde's coachman, whom Blood had failed to tie up, raced to Clarendon House, warning that his master had been seized and carried down Portugal Street. A chase was immediately made, and the game old Duke, who had somehow loosened his bonds, was discovered in a violent struggle in the winter mud with the villain he had been tied to – who then regained his horse, fired a badly aimed pistol at the Duke, and made his escape.

The Duke's injuries, described by his doctor as a bruised eye and cut head, kept him only a few days in bed. The indomitable Blood also lived to fight on. A year later he was plotting the theft of the Crown Jewels and Regalia – but that is another story.

Quite apart from this unfortunate incident, Ormonde was, at the time he lived in Clarendon House, an unhappy man. Having achieved greatness at court in the days of Charles I, he was, in the new world of Charles II, out of date. Though the new King always treated his father's old ally with respect, he preferred to have new people around him: Ormonde's ancient nobility fatigued him.

No happy person ever possessed Clarendon House. Shortly after the death of Clarendon in exile, his sons sold the house to Christopher, the 2nd and last Duke of Albemarle, a spendthrift and drunkard, for £26,000, on July 10th, 1675, after which it became known as Albemarle House. New Letters Patent were granted, dated November 10th, 1677, ratifying the ground to him and his heirs and assigns for ever. Lord Clarendon's lease of the Conduit Mead also passed to the Duke.

The young Albemarle, however, appears soon to have run through his father's money (Evelyn refers to the "prodigious waste of his estate"), and in 1683 he was forced to sell Albemarle House to the highest bidder, a syndicate of contractors.

Having ruined his health by excessive drinking, being "burnt to a coal with hot liquor", Albemarle was subsequently sent out to Jamaica as Governor, the young Hans Sloane accompanying him as medical attendant. Albemarle's only real aim in undertaking this office was, it seems, to weigh up a rich Spanish galleon which had sunk off the island, and this enterprise was apparently successful: exaggerated rumours of his having discovered a silver mine soon leaked back to England. He, however, died in 1688, before he could return home, and his widow is said to have cheated the other partners in the scheme and brought all the loot to England. She went mad, declaring that she would marry none but the Emperor of China. Ralph, the 1st Duke of Montague, wooed and married her in that disguise, then promptly had her confined and made use of her money to build Montague House, afterwards the British Museum.

When Albemarle House was sold, the Duke had, according to Evelyn in a diary entry for September 18th, 1683, been successful in making a considerable profit by the sale. "Certain rich bankers and merchants," he tells us, "gave for it, and the ground about it, £35,000. They design a new town, as it were, and a most magnificent piazza. 'Tis said they have already materials towards it with what they sold of the house alone, more worth than what they paid for it, and a little army of labourers and artificers levelling the ground, laying founda-

13

tions, and contriving great buildings, at an expense of £200,000, if they perfect their design." Evelyn naturally regretted the destruction of the mansion so soon after it had been built; he had been greatly interested in its construction, himself helping to plan the gardens and build up the collection of portraits for the state rooms.

"I returned to town with the Earl of Clarendon," writes Evelyn that same year, "when, passing by the glorious palace his father had built but a few years before, which they were now demolishing . . . I turned my head the contrary way till the coach was gone past it, lest I might minister occasion of speaking of it, which must needs have grieved him that in so short a time their pomp was so sadly fallen."

The syndicate referred to by Evelyn as "certain rich bankers and merchants" was headed by a wealthy goldsmith and banker, John Hinde. Also associated in the venture were Cadogan Thomas, a timber merchant and land speculator, and Richard Frith, a building contractor already at work in the new St James's Square. Clarendon House was demolished. The project began auspiciously because, as Evelyn notes, the £35,000 paid for it was recovered by the sale of old materials alone. Building leases of various parts of the land which had been occupied by Clarendon House were granted, three of the major leaseholders being Sir Thomas Bond, Harry Jermyn and Margaret Stafford. On the site of the mansion were built Bond, Albemarle, Dover and Stafford Streets, though the whole of the development was for a time known as Albemarle Buildings. John Evelyn was to take a house in Dover Street in 1699, where he died on February 27th, 1706.

Sir Thomas Bond, one of the major leaseholders in this important building operation, was a devoted follower of Charles II, to whom, when in exile, he had advanced large sums of money, and by whom he was created a baronet in 1658. He was Comptroller of the Household to Queen Henrietta Maria, the Queen Mother, both abroad and after the Restoration. He was well to the fore in the glad celebrations when Charles was returned to the throne: indeed in the procession which entered London he was at his monarch's side. He is mentioned in the diaries of Pepys and Evelyn, but his name lives chiefly in the great street which was called after him and after which so many other streets aspiring to worth have been named. He did not live long after the purchase of Albemarle House, but died in his fine house at Peckham in 1685, the year before Old Bond Street was actually laid out, and was buried at Camberwell.

Work on Albemarle Buildings began bravely. The site of the mansion was covered by four streets, three turning out of Portugal Street: Bond Street (this being only the short stretch of Old Bond Street, running into open country where New Bond Street was later to be built), Albemarle Street, named after the last possessor of the house, and Dover Street, named after leaseholder Harry Jermyn, the Earl of Dover, nephew and heir of Henry Jermyn, the Earl of St Albans. The fourth street, running across at right angles from Dover Street, through Albemarle Street to Bond Street, was Stafford Street, named after Margaret Stafford, another of the leaseholders.

The piazza mentioned by Evelyn was to have been a three-acre square – Albemarle Square – immediately to the north of Old Bond, Albemarle and Dover Streets. However, by this time the contractors were in financial difficulties and the idea had to be abandoned. The land which was to have been occupied by the square was later sold to the Duke of Grafton and other residents of the northern extremes of Bond, Albemarle and Dover Streets, who were anxious to preserve an area of open space on their doorsteps. However, it was not long before the building of streets was extended northwards, the Duke himself being immortalised by Grafton Street.

The Albemarle Buildings project was soon to bring financial ruin to its instigators. It was a great many years before the original plans for the wider district were to take even partial shape. In 1685 John Hinde was imprisoned for bankruptcy, being, according to some reports, £200,000 in debt. He died in the Fleet prison a year and a half later, a few months after Sir Thomas Bond. Though the fine street which was to immortalise Bond was still to arise from the ashes of Albemarle House, he had also not done well from the Albemarle Buildings project: when he died a number of houses had already been built on his plots, but only one of these was occupied, the rest being heavily mortgaged. Hinde's associates, Cadogan Thomas and Richard Frith lived on into the next decade but were also hounded by debtors.

From 1683 John Hinde's syndicate, already at work on Albemarle Buildings, was faced also with trouble of another sort. Residents south of Piccadilly complained to the Commissioner of Sewers for Westminster that drains from the new houses were being allowed to flow into the Tyburn, then an open stream, and they feared that they would "be drownded in their houses upon any great rain", for the channel under the stone bridge over Piccadilly was not wide enough to carry all the rain and waste water. Drainage, in subsequent years, remained a problem, holding up building works, although a new sewer was built. In 1686 the contractors were again accused of connecting their drains with the Tyburn so that "great quantities of soil and filth flowed into the fresh water."

Berkeley and Stratton Streets were built about the same time as those on the site of Albemarle House, on land to the north of Berkeley House which was sold to building contractors by Lord Berkeley's widow. Berkeley House had been built by Sir John Berkeley, later created Lord Berkeley of Stratton, to the west of Clarendon House in 1665, on land which had been part of Hay Hill Farm. Though palatial, and though designed by a friend of his, Hugh May, it did not impress that excellent critic of art and architecture, John Evelyn, as had Clarendon House. In his diary he describes a visit to Lord Berkeley's "new house, or rather Palace, for I am assured it stood him in near £30,000. It is very well built, and has many noble rooms, but they are not very convenient, consisting but of one *Corps de Logis*; they are all rooms of state, without closets." It was usual for great houses of the time to offer grandeur rather than comfort. Pope endorsed Evelyn's doubts about such houses in his couplet:

> Thanks, sir, cried I, 'tis very fine,
> But where d'ye sleep, or where d'ye dine?

In another contemporary account, the house is described as being "built of brick, adorned with stone pilasters and an entablature and pitched pediment, all of the Corinthian order . . ." There were majestic curved wings on both sides of the main building, consisting of stables and domestic offices, connected to the central section of the mansion by "brick walls, and two circular galleries, each elevated on columns of the Corinthian order, where are two ambulatories."

Lord Berkeley died in 1678 and six years later his widow approached her friend John Evelyn for advice about selling some of her land for development. The grounds of Berkeley House extended northwards to where Berkeley Square and its surrounding streets were later to be built. After her discussion with Evelyn, Lady Berkeley sold much of this land to developers, though she continued to live in the house. Evelyn tells us in his diary what he did, but makes it quite plain that he regretted the building of these streets. He writes: "June 12, 1684. I went to advise and give directions about the building two streets in Berkeley Gardens, reserving the house and as much of the garden as the breadth of the house. In the meantime I could not but deplore that sweet place (by far the most noble gardens, courts and accommodations, stately porticos, &c, anywhere about the town) should be so much straitened and turned into tenements. But that magnificent pile and gardens contiguous to it, built by the late Lord Chancellor Clarendon, being all demolished, and designed for piazzas and buildings, was some excuse for my Lady Berkeley's resolution of letting out her ground, also for so excessive a price as was offered, advancing near £1000 per annum in mere ground rents; to such a mad intemperance was the age come of building about a City by far too disproportionate already to the nation; I having in my time seen it almost as large again as it was within my memory."

Berkeley House itself was later occupied by Princess Anne, the sister of Queen Mary, and her husband, the amiable, alcoholic Prince George of Denmark, after a quarrel with the King and Queen. When Mary died, however, King William made overtures of friendship, offering Anne St James's Palace. In the spring of 1696 she departed from Berkeley House.

At the beginning of 1697 the house was bought by William Cavendish, the 1st Duke of Devonshire, after which it was called Devonshire House. It became a fashionable resort for the cream of society, splendidly opening its doors for the entertainment of ambassadors and kings. In October 1733, in the day of the 3rd Duke, the mansion was completely destroyed by fire. Within weeks, however, plans were in operation for a new Devonshire House, begun in 1736 on open ground to the north which was later to be developed into Berkeley Square. The new Devonshire House survived into the twentieth century on the south side of Berkeley Square.

Years of tortuous litigation followed the death of John Hinde as an attempt was made to establish the ownership of the various new properties on the site of Albemarle House and also on the newly developed grounds of Berkeley House, a complex matter since boundaries had seldom been properly defined. Though the houses in Old Bond Street and the other streets in the southern part of the Albemarle Buildings development were soon completed and occupied by the gentry and aristocracy, many houses to the north of these streets, some finished, others only half built, were left to fall into disrepair as, twenty years after Hinde's death, they were still unoccupied and Hinde's affairs still under arbitration.

Soon after 1700 Bond Street had been extended from Burlington Gardens as far as Clifford Street, the extension being named New Bond Street. The original street was renamed Old Bond Street.

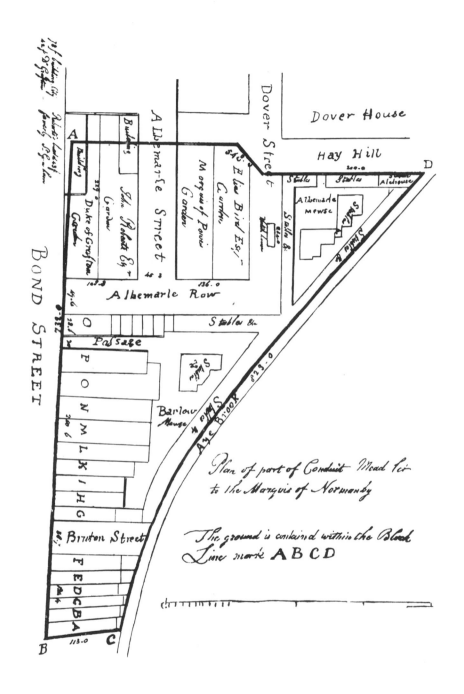

Plan of part of the Conduit Mead, c.1721, showing the early
development of New Bond Street

19

In 1711, by which time Old Bond Street was already "a fine new street, mostly inhabited by nobility and gentry," the area of New Bond Street between Clifford Street and Oxford Street, was, in the words of Hunter's *History of London*, "still an open field, called Conduit Mead, from one of the conduits which supplied that part of the town with water, and from which Conduit Street, adjoining, derived its name. All beyond was open ground, a receptacle for dunghills, and every kind of refuse . . . Oxford Street was then built on the south side, as far as Swallow Street (now absorbed in Regent Street), but almost unbuilt on the north side. It was a deep hollow road full of sloughs, with here and there a ragged house, the lurking place of cut-throats."

In 1721 the extension of New Bond Street from Clifford Street to Oxford Street was laid out by the Earl of Oxford. The earliest portion of New Bond Street was in St Martin's parish, but the further extension over the Conduit Mead was a portion of the parish of St George's, Hanover Square. The parish church of St George had been recently consecrated in 1716. It was not long before this became one of the richest livings in London; it was a highly fashionable church for sumptuous weddings. The whole area was developing quickly at this time and complaints were soon being made about new buildings pushing in too closely around the church.

The speed of the changes was felt by James Brampton:

Peese, cabbages and turnips once grew, where
Now stands New Bond Street and a newer square

he rhymed in 1729. The square was Grosvenor Square, built in 1725. Sir Richard Grosvenor had hoped to make Grosvenor Street one of the great streets of London, leading straight to the east with a direct view of St George's Church, in St George's Street, at its end. However, the planning of his estate, which ended to the west of Bond Street, and the Conduit Mead Estate further east were not co-ordinated and when

20

Maddox Street was laid out as a continuation of Hanover Street, it was not in a perfectly straight line, and blocked the view of the church.

The history of the Conduit Mead Estate is an interesting one, though it is too large a subject to be fully detailed here. When the city granted long leases of this estate to Lord Clarendon, and, later, to Lord Mulgrave, the property was of little value, but, with the growth of the West End, it very soon became most valuable, and the Corporation lost a considerable income for many years.

The Clarendon lease of the Conduit Mead had been, as already stated, transferred to the Duke of Albemarle, though it is not certain how far the contractors who bought Clarendon House became interested in this lease. In 1723 the scheme for building on the Conduit Mead was brought to a satisfactory conclusion. This is fully related in a curious and scarce tract published in 1743, entitled "An Examination of the Conduct of several Comptrollers of the City of London, in relation to the City's Estate call'd Conduit Mead, now New Bond Street, &c, wherein the reasoning of those Officers to induce the City to let new leases thereof *now*, being upwards of twenty years before the expiration of the present lease, is refuted, and the true design of the whole disclosed." This tract was reprinted in the following year, being further described as "The City-Secret; or Corruption at all ends of the Town; containing a succinct History of an 100,000*l* jobb . . ."

The main point of the information in this pamphlet is as follows: "Conduit Mead is situated in the Parish of St George, Hanover Square, in Middlesex, and was formerly an open field containing 27 acres, and continued so till about 1716, when the Lord Burlington, having set on foot a considerable building in parts adjacent to this Mead, the Lessees of the Mead began to think of building there, and finding Lord Burlington's scheme to prove beneficial, they began to put their design in execution, and in a short time, out of an open field, raised those streets and Buildings now call'd New Bond Street, Conduit Street, Brook Street, Woodstock Street, Silver Street, Great George

21

Burlington House, 1707, to the left of which is seen part of the undeveloped Conduit Mead

Street, Pedley Street, South Molton Row and Lancashire Court, which at present consist of 429 houses, all, except a very few, extremely well built, 21 Stable yards, and 15 vacant pieces of ground, the annual rent wherof now is, according to a particular in the Comptroller's office, 14,240*l* 15*s* 0*d*, being altogether one of the best conditioned estates in the Country."

The writer then proceeds to give the particulars as to the leases by which the city had been such heavy losers. "Of this estate the City is seized in Fee, which they hold by a possession from time out of mind, so clear and uninterrupted that no person has, in the memory or to the knowledge of any man living, ever pretended any right to the same, save what they claim under the City's leases, of which there are but two subsisting – the one was granted for 99 years at eight pounds a year, which expires 7th of March, 1765, and the other 13th of December, 1694, to the then Lord Mulgrave, of a parcel of this Mead containing four acres, two roods and thirty-seven poles, for one hundred years from the expiration of the Lease before mentioned, to Lord Clarendon, at the yearly rent of two pounds. On this part of the estate the improvements amount to 1,778*l* 10*s* a year, so that by granting this second lease the City hath lost an estate of 1,776*l* a year for 40*s*, and are in a fair way, if the scheme which is now on foot should prevail, of losing the remaining 12,465*l* 5*s* 0*d* a year for a very little better consideration."

At the time of the building of Clarendon House and Berkeley House, Burlington House was erected to the east of them by Sir John Denham, another unhappy follower of Charles II. In about 1665, "loaded with wealth as well as years" (he was, in fact, only fifty) he had married the nineteen-year-old court debutante, Margaret Brook, who became the mistress of the Duke of York. She did not live long, though long enough to see her suffering husband depart temporarily from his reason (on one occasion he sought out His Majesty and assured him that he was the Holy Ghost). Denham was the King's Surveyor-

General until losing his position to Christopher Wren, though now better remembered for his poetry than his architecture. He recovered his wits sufficiently to produce some more fine verse, but did not long survive his young wife.

It is not certain whether Sir John Denham ever lived in Burlington House, or ever meant to, it being somewhat grandiose for one in his position. It may from the beginning have been intended for Richard Boyle, the 1st Earl of Burlington: in any case, by 1668, and for the next thirty years, this was Lord Burlington's London home.

The house had been built between the years 1664 and 1667; the architect, working under Denham's direction, was John Webb, pupil of Inigo Jones. Built of red brick, the house appears to have been large and comfortable. It was arranged on two main floors, with an attic floor, and had slightly projecting wings to either side of a central section. There was a courtyard in front, facing on to Piccadilly, on either side of which were outbuildings, a high brick wall and trees protecting it from the public road. The extensive gardens behind the house were laid out with formal hedges and small cropped trees, and fruit trees round the walls. They extended back to what is now the end of Savile Row and what was then the open Conduit Mead. A court by the side of the house, called Savile Place, led through into Mill Street and Conduit Street: it was originally a pathway to St George's church. Beyond the garden wall at the back were fields, in one of which stood Trinity Chapel. This was originally erected on wheels at the camp at Hounslow Heath, in the reign of James II, and in it Mass was daily performed. In 1688 the chapel was removed to this spot and reconsecrated for the Protestant service. In 1725, when Conduit Street was built, a new chapel was erected on its south side.

In 1718, about fifty years after it was first built, Burlington House was extensively altered by the 3rd Earl of Burlington, who was the last of his line – after his death in 1753 the house passing to the Cavendish family, relatives by marriage. A new coating of stone entirely changed the south front of Burlington House. This work, the great gate and the street wall were done by Colin Campbell, but the beautiful colonnade which was built at the same time, and was so well proportioned that Sir William Chambers considered it and the house as specimens of one of the finest pieces of architecture in Europe, is attributed to the Earl of Burlington himself. A great deal of money was spent on the alterations and Burlington indulged heavily in lavish hospitality: he soon found it necessary, for financial reasons, to develop the land to the back of the house, and here arose, between 1716 and 1718, more well-designed houses of high fashion. It was the laying out of Burlington and Cork Streets that led to the extension of New Bond Street to Oxford Street, over a portion of the Conduit Mead. One of the streets to be built, in about 1716, on land which had been part of the Burlington House estate was Vigo Lane, leading from Swallow Street (afterwards developed into Regent Street) into Bond Street. It was named Vigo Lane in honour of the action at Vigo Bay in 1702, but was later re-named Burlington Gardens.

At the time of the first building of Bond Street, the turnpike in Portugal Street (Piccadilly) was situated to the east of Berkeley Street. Beyond was the Great Western Road, entirely unpaved. The turnpike was removed to Hyde Park Corner in 1721. Roads, especially the Great Western Road, were very bad, and coaches were frequently overturned or stopped by highwaymen; conditions in the area remained hazardous well into the eighteenth century, years after Bond Street, both Old and New, was laid out.

In 1692 Sir Robert Atkyns, Lord Chief Baron of the Exchequer and Speaker of the House of Lords, who lived two miles out of town at Kensington, failed on March 1st, the day appointed for a conference between the Lords and Commons, to make his appearance, owing to "the badness of the roads", and the Lords were obliged to choose a temporary Speaker.

The Western Road did not quickly improve. Lord Hervey, writing to his mother from Kensington in November 1736, says: "The road between this place and London is grown so infamously bad that we live here in the same solitude as we should do if cast on a rock in the middle of the ocean, and all the Londoners tell us there is between them and us a great, impassable gulf of mud. There are two roads through the park, but the new one is so convex and the old one so concave, that by this extreme of faults they agree in the common one of being, like the high road, impassable."

Complaints were made about flooding after heavy rains in the unfortunate hollow occupied by the Marquis of Hertford's mansion at 105 Piccadilly. In December 1726 the carriage of the Ambassador of Morocco was overturned and his daughter almost killed. The author of a *History and Present State of the British Isles* (1743) refers to the same state of things. He writes: "This being one of the great roads from Exeter and the West of England, the pavement is, for the most part, miserably broken and hazardous to ride upon, as it is in most of the streets leading to the great roads."

Horace Walpole, writing in 1750, says that, as he was sitting in his dining-room in Arlington Street, one night at eleven o'clock, he heard a loud cry of "Stop thief!" On enquiry he found that a highwayman had attacked a post-chaise in Piccadilly, not fifty yards from his house, and adds that, although the attempt was unsuccessful, the man escaped. To bring the record of the insecurity of the neighbourhood a little nearer to Bond Street itself, it may be recorded that, at the end of the seventeenth century, a thief who had stolen a silver mug from the house of the great physician, Dr Sydenham, in Pall Mall, got away and was lost in the bushes on the Conduit Mead.

Petty theft there was, of course, always in abundance, and not all the thieves managed to make their escapes. J. T. Smith, in his *Book for a Rainy Day*, amusingly recalls how, in a later incident, he once saw Dr Johnson "follow a sturdy thief, who had stolen his handkerchief in Grosvenor Square, seize him by the collar with both hands, and

26

shake him violently, after which he quickly let him loose; and then with his open hand, give him so powerful a smack on the face, that sent him off the pavement, staggering."

Such, then, was the condition, in the seventeenth and earlier part of the eighteenth centuries, of the neighbourhood of Bond Street, when it was already a place of distinction and special interest.

Chapter Two

GEORGIAN BOND STREET

*   *   *

The Restoration noblemen who built their mansions along Piccadilly early on set the tone of the embryonic Mayfair: when the streets between Piccadilly and Oxford Street later came to be laid out they immediately constituted a desirable neighbourhood. According to the *Weekly Journal* in the summer of 1717, "The new buildings between Bond Street and Mary-le-bone go on with all possible diligence and the houses even let and sell before they are built. They are already in great forwardness."

Bond Street was from the beginning in the heart of a prestigious neighbourhood. In 1708 Hatton, in his *New View of London*, described it as "a fine street, mostly inhabited by nobility and gentry." Bond Street has never, however, been noted for architectural splendour: an extract from *A Critical Review of the Public Buildings of London* (1736) is most uncomplimentary about it: "There is nothing in the whole prodigious length of the two Bond Streets or in any of the adjacent places, though almost all erected within our memories, that has anything worth our attention; several little wretched attempts there are at foppery in building, but they are too inconsiderable even for censure." The writer was not to guess that in the course of a few years Bond Street was to become one of the most fashionable streets of London and that its shops were to be the most important emporium of articles of beauty and taste.

Nevertheless, at this time and for a long while afterwards, the elegance of Mayfair was interspersed with squalor: beyond the fine new houses of Bond Street was a jumble of unplanned little streets of tiny houses occupied by tradesmen and artisans serving their wealthy neighbours. James Boswell's *London Journal* of the 1760s includes the following interesting observation about the squares of Mayfair: "Behind these gracious houses, however, with no gardens to insulate them, were closely-ranged houses and tenements of a baser sort, so that the back windows of 'the Squares' looked out on a sordid prospect and were looked in upon by many pairs of eyes, some envious, some hostile . . ." Even in Victorian times this disparity still existed in Mayfair.

John Rocque's map of Mayfair of 1747 already shows the streets of Mayfair as we know them today, although the area was then not yet completely built up. Up till 1783 the gallows still stood near the turnpike where present-day Park Lane, then Tyburn Lane, a little-used country track, joins Oxford Street – which in Rocque's map is indicated as Tyburn Road to the west of New Bond Street and Oxford Road to the east. Public executions of course took place at Tyburn as long as the gallows were there: in 1769 James Boswell saw "the execution of several convicts" and remarked to Dr Johnson that "none of them seemed to be under any concern". Johnson's caustic reply was that "Most of them, Sir, have never thought at all." After the disappearance of the gibbet the development of the area around Grosvenor Square was completed and Park Lane came into being. At the date of the map Regent Street had not yet been built and Great Swallow Street (later largely replaced by Regent Street) is shown as the eastern boundary of Mayfair, connected to New Bond Street by Conduit Street.

The three chief streets built upon the site of Clarendon or Albemarle House were at first inhabited by persons of quality in large private houses. These original late-seventeenth-century buildings of Bond Street and its neighbours were large, four-storeyed brick houses, no doubt plain and unpretentious, as houses of the period tended to be, but with a fine dignity of proportion. It was not long before an increasing number of ground floors came to be occupied by shops so that gradually Bond Street became a principal place of business, filled with shops and lodging houses, while Albemarle and Dover Streets remained much longer streets of private residences. The shopkeepers of Bond Street would usually live over their own shops, letting off extra rooms to lodgers of means who wished to maintain some sort of fashionable presence in town without incurring the expense of running a fashionable house. Many of the distinguished people who lived here were birds of passage who used their lodgings for only a short time. Some of the more illustrious members of society of the day would give as their addresses the upper parts of Bond Street shops and one comes across references to such as the "Duke of A, at Mr Jones's, hairdressers" or, as in the address of a letter Dr Johnson wrote from Lichfield in 1767, "To Bennet Langton, Esq. at Mr Rothwell's, Perfumer, in New Bond Street, London." These were usefully specific descriptions in the days before street numbering.

One of the early titled inhabitants of Bond Street was Charles Beauclerk, the Duke of St Albans, elder son of Charles II and Nell Gwynn. His earlier title, Earl of Burford, was, according to the story, something of a royal afterthought. The King one day, overhearing the child's mother call him – no doubt for some good reason – "little bastard", objected to this form of address to his offspring. Nell assured him that it was apt as the unfortunate boy had no other title. Shortly afterwards a patent of nobility was made out for him. After Henry Jermyn, the old Earl of St Albans, who had been one of the developers of Albemarle Buildings, died, his lapsed title passed to the King's son in 1685, Harry Jermyn, the nephew and heir of the old Earl of St Albans, and one of the Albemarle Buildings leaseholders after whom Dover Street was named, being made the 1st Baron Dover. The Duke of St Albans probably came to Bond Street in about 1720, and died here in 1726. The following year his house was advertised in *The London*

Gazette: "To be let or sold . . . A House in Old Bond Street, Piccadilly, of four rooms on a floor, with closets, good cellar and all other conveniences. Being the house in which the late Duke of St Albans lived. Inquire at the Said House." The house was taken for one year by the Duchess of Kendal, mistress of George I, after George's death and before she moved to Grosvenor Square in 1728.

The important members of the aristocracy who lived in Bond Street in Georgian times, and who are now naturally largely forgotten, are too numerous to mention, though a few may be singled out. The enthusiastic John Macky, fresh from Scotland and staggered by London, gives us an interesting and appreciative description of Paulet's house and Bond Street in general in his curious *Journey Through England* (1714): "The Earl Paulet," he writes, "late Lord Steward of the Household, hath a most magnificent Palace at the end of Bond Street, with a fine prospect to the adjacent country, and indeed all Bond Street are palaces; the Earls of Orkney, Portmore and many others of the nobility have sumptuous lodgings all round that quarter." This was of course before the building of New Bond Street.

The 2nd and 3rd Dukes of Grafton lived at Grafton House in New Bond Street during the middle of the eighteenth century: the 3rd Duke's mistress, the notorious Nancy Parsons, was the daughter of a Bond Street tailor. Though really in New Bond Street, Grafton House was situated near the north end of Old Bond Street and George Selwyn described himself, in 1751, as living in "lodgings opposite the Duke of Grafton's in Old Bond Street." Later Grafton House was occupied by the Earl of Chatham, who will be discussed presently. When Grafton House was pulled down, Grafton Street was built, partly on the site of the house and partly on Ducking Pond Row.

Marriages between lords and actresses or other desirable commoners were not considered unacceptable in the eighteenth century so that the catalogue of members of the aristocracy has some interesting inclusions. The actress Lavinia Fenton, who later became the Duchess of Bolton, lived in Bond Street in 1730: it was she who immortalised the character of Polly Peachum in John Gay's *Beggar's Opera*. Lord Coventry, who later married one of the beautiful but lowly Gunnings, was in New Bond Street in 1732. The two Irish-bred girls, the toast of London, were married within weeks of each other in 1752, both to members of the aristocracy. Elizabeth, the younger, married the Duke of Hamilton at the little Mayfair Chapel in Curzon Street where over a period some seven thousand marriages were clandestinely performed, in a similar way to those at Gretna Green and the Fleet Prison. There was no licence, publication of banns or consent of parents, but though such marriages were irregular, provided the parson had taken holy orders, they were considered valid and binding.

After a lightning courtship by the Duke of Hamilton, including making violent love during an assembly held at the house of Lord Chesterfield, two nights later Hamilton impatiently decided to get married, while Elizabeth's mother and sister were absent. It is recorded by Horace Walpole that the Duke went through the ceremony "with a ring of the bed-curtain, at half an hour after twelve at night"! Such marriages were outlawed two years later, yet on the very day before the new Act came into force sixty-one couples were married in the little unpretending chapel. In 1758 the Duke died, and his widow later that year removed to New Bond Street, marrying, the following February, Colonel John Campbell, son of the heir to the 3rd Duke of Argyll. Her husband became the 5th Duke in 1770. Elizabeth's first two children were born at Holyrood Palace; after she remarried, she gave birth to a girl at her home in Bond Street in March 1760, and here again to a boy in February 1763, though he died a year later. Curiously enough, at the end of her life, when in Naples, she met and befriended a later inhabitant of Bond Street, the mistress of Sir William Hamilton, and it has been said that, if it had not been for the patronage of the Duchess, there would have been no Emma, Lady Hamilton.

Towards the end of the eighteenth century the Duchess of Devonshire is said to have played an important part in popularising Bond Street with those in the forefront of fashion. She had lived in Covent Garden, in Tavistock Street, then a most fashionable address, but was so incensed by the fact that most of the people of that district voted against Fox, for whom she had canvassed in the Westminster election of 1784, that she moved to Bond Street, and proceeded to draw after her the cream of people of rank from Covent Garden.

The aristocracy apart, the list of famous eighteenth-century people who have actually lived in Bond Street is a most interesting one. Richard West, the poet and friend of Gray, was studying for the Bar at the Inner Temple in 1733, but left it for lodgings in Bond Street, telling Gray, "I lived in the Temple till I was sick of it. It is certain at least that I can study the law here as well as I could there." And the arts are well represented by others too.

James Thomson (1700–48), the poet of the *Seasons*, took lodgings with a milliner at 141 New Bond Street before departing for the rich pastures of "ambrosial Richmond". (The same house was, later in the century, occupied by Lord Nelson. Later demolished, its site is now covered by the present No. 147.) Born and educated in Scotland, he had begun at an early age to write poetry on rustic themes – poetry which was, in the full flower of its development, to herald a new era in English literature with its natural and romantic treatment of nature. Seeking his fortune in London in 1725, Thomson wrote the first of his seasons, "Winter", before he had found it, and while still impecunious. The milder seasons followed in the next five years, bringing deserved renown and its rewards. However, perhaps the best-known of Thomson's compositions was to be that "noble ode" better remembered than his name, "Rule Britannia", which, in the words of Southey, is destined to be "the political hymn of this country as long as she maintains her political power".

It was Lord Beaconsfield who once expressed the view that "Those who know Bond Street only in the blaze of fashionable hours can form but an imperfect conception of its matutinal charm when it is still shady and fresh, when there are no carriages, rarely a cart, and passers-by gliding about on real business." To Thomson, however, the charm of such an hour must have been unknown as Mrs Piozzi, satirising the nature poet, remarked: "So charming Thomson writes from his lodgings at a milliner's in Bond Street, where he seldom rises early enough to see the sun do more than glisten on the opposite windows of the streets." Though his rising at noon was a result of his energetically working all through the night, he did have a reputation for indolence and epicureanism. The traditional picture of the amiable, lazy, over-weight poet eating "the sunny side off the peaches in his garden with his hands in his pockets" is perhaps contradicted by his active life.

Jonathan Swift (1667–1745), the prolific writer and satirist and great Dean of St Patrick's, best known today for his *Gulliver's Travels*, spent three weeks in New Bond Street at his cousin Lancelot's house "over against the Crown and Cushion". He came here on August 31st, 1727, after hurriedly leaving Pope's house at Twickenham, and after his brief stay left England forever, returning to Ireland where his beloved Stella was dying.

Mrs Delany, that delightfully garrulous writer of memoirs, lived in Bond Street in 1731, when she was Mrs Pendarves, before marrying Dr Patrick Delany. A friend of Jonathan Swift, Queen Charlotte, Fanny Burney (whom she introduced at court) and many other eighteenth-century notables, her indefatigible writings cast a revealing light on the social life of her times.

George Selwyn (1719–91), the politician and wit, lived in Bond Street in 1751. A man with apparently irreconcilable characteristics – he was graciously tender to children and morbidly fascinated by death and human suffering – he is remembered for his wit and not his politics. As a Member of Parliament he is said to have snored through debates in the House for fifty years; on the other hand he was celebrated as the wittiest man of his time and a foremost dandy, addicted to the frivolous

Jonathan Swift, who spent his last three weeks in England in New Bond Street in 1727

Edward Gibbon, a Bond Street lodger in 1758, during an unhappy period of his youth

Lord Chatham, the illustrious occupier of Grafton House in New Bond Street in 1766

Laurence Sterne the humorist, who died a lonely death in Old Bond Street lodgings in 1768

35

pleasures of velvets, muffs and fans. A brilliant conversationalist, he was much in demand round the dinner table, which he could always manage to keep convulsed in a roar of laughter, while his genial witticisms were joyfully repeated throughout the town. Not his best, but one of his most celebrated remarks was in answer to his friend Horace Walpole's complaint that politics had not advanced at all since Queen Anne's day. Walpole sighed fatalistically, "But there is nothing new under the sun." To which Selwyn immediately threw back, "Nor under the grandson!" – referring to George III.

Selwyn's passion for executions took him frequently to Tyburn: on one occasion a friend is said to have wagered a hundred guineas that he would not be able to keep away from Tyburn on the day a man was to be hanged. Though Selwyn naughtily accepted the bet, he was discovered lurking in the crowd dressed as an old apple-woman and lost his money. When a man with the same name as Charles James Fox was hanged at Tyburn, the more illustrious Fox asked Selwyn if he had been there. "No," replied Selwyn, "I never go to rehearsals."

One of the aristocratic inhabitants of Bond Street was the Countess of Macclesfield, who died here in 1753. Her unfortunate notoriety in the literary world was almost certainly based on a misapprehension. The minor poet Richard Savage, who had been much under the influence of the better work of James Thomson, and who had died ten years before the Countess, claimed to have been the illegitimate son of the 4th Earl Rivers and the Countess of Macclesfield – a romantic story of shady birth and desertion told by Samuel Johnson in his *Life* of the poet. Though the story is now discounted and Savage assumed to have been of humble birth, it is quite likely that he had himself fully believed his assertions: his poem "The Bastard" censures his supposed mother.

The venerable historian Edward Gibbon (1737–94) lodged for a while in Bond Street when young and fresh from Lausanne, where he had been painstakingly cured of his brief flirtation with Catholicism, and suffered the one romance of his life. The former achieved, the latter showing itself as a problem, he had been summoned home in 1758: "I sighed as a lover," says he much later in his *Autobiography*, "I obeyed as a son."

The lovesick boy found little to enjoy in London, which to him seemed to offer only "crowds without company, and dissipation without pleasure." He lived in the midst of the fashionable world, but, making few friends, studied in the quiet of his own rooms: "I had not been endowed by art or nature with those happy gifts of confidence and address which unlock every door and every bosom," he wrote, "nor would it be reasonable to complain of the just consequences of my sickly childhood, foreign education, and reserved temper. While coaches were rattling through Bond Street, I have passed many solitary evenings in my lodgings with my books." It was not until 1772, when he returned to London after another trip to Europe, that he began work on his great *Decline and Fall of the Roman Empire*.

The great orator and statesman William Pitt the elder, 1st Earl of Chatham (1708–78) was in Bond Street in 1766. The giant of a politician, of haughty and irreproachable character, imposing appearance and magnificent voice, had, by this time, lived through the greatest moments of his illustrious career. He had won fame, a comfortable pension of £3,000 a year and, in this year of 1766, an Earldom, but was now in failing health. In 1766 he formed a new ministry, a heterogeneous administration composed of "patriots and courtiers, king's friends and republicans", but chose for himself the minor office of privy seal, almost a sinecure, with a seat in the House of Lords. He was now too ill to exert much influence on his inept ministry, or to make frequent public appearances. Two years later he was to resign. It was in Grafton House that Boswell – who will get a good mention in his own right a little later – in Corsican dress and with a letter from Paoli in his hand, was introduced to the great Earl of Chatham to plead the cause of Corsica.

Archibald Bower (1686–1766), the Scottish, ex-Jesuit author of the great *History of the Popes*, died in Bond Street in September 1766 at a ripe old age.

Not long afterwards Laurence Sterne, the humorist and sentimentalist, author of that whimsical expression of his own personality and imagination, *Tristram Shandy*, died at 41 Old Bond Street. This was on March 18th, 1768, and in lodgings over what was then a silk-bag shop (in the mid-nineteenth century it was a "Cheesemonger's shop", while later that century the site of this building was occupied by the premises of Agnew's New Art Gallery).

Not long before, Sterne had returned from Yorkshire "to his lodgings in Bond Street, with", in the words of Thackeray, "his *Sentimental Journey* to launch upon the town, eager as ever for praise and pleasure, as vain, as wicked, as witty, and as false as he had ever been, when death seized the feeble wretch." *Sentimental Journey*, a rosy narrative of his travels in France in 1765–6, published at the end of February, made a tremendous sensation. Visitors flocked to his lodgings in Bond Street to applaud him and even Horace Walpole, who had found the recurring volumes of "Shandy" so "tiresome" was ready to admit that Sterne's new book was "very pleasing though too much dilated" and that it contained "great good nature and strokes of delicacy". However, though his name was a household word and his books were in every hand, Sterne was, at the end of his life, poor, if not actually in debt. Before leaving town on his "Sentimental Journey" he had written to Garrick begging the loan of £10.

A few days after his return to London, Sterne wrote to his daughter, complaining of a vile influenza which was afflicting him. "I wish I had thee to nurse me," he wrote, "but I am denied that. Write to me twice a week at least." His condition rapidly deteriorated and pleurisy set in. He was bled and blistered and grew weaker and weaker. Four days before he died he wrote poignantly to his friend Mrs James of Gerrard Street in Soho, asking her to take care of his daughter should he not come through his illness. It was the last thing he ever wrote. "My spirits are fled," he said, "'tis a bad omen."

On the afternoon of Friday, March 18th, Sterne's friend John Crawford was giving a party for a company of distinguished guests, including Garrick, David Hume and other friends and patrons of Sterne, in Clifford Street close by. Concerned for his friend, Crawford dispatched his Scottish footman, James Macdonald, to the sick man's lodgings to enquire after him, and Macdonald, who later published his memoirs, has left the following description of the strange last scene that occurred at four o'clock that afternoon: "About this time Mr Sterne, the celebrated author, was taken ill at the silk-bag shop in Old Bond Street . . . I went to Mr Sterne's lodgings; the mistress opened the door; I inquired how he did. She told me to go up to the nurse; I went into the room, and he was just a-dying. I waited ten minutes; but in five he said, 'Now it is come'! He put up his hand as if to stop a blow, and died in a minute." The lodging-house servant, his only nurse, is said by Dr Ferriar, his medical attendant, to have torn the gold buttons from his sleeves as he lay dying. He died insolvent and his wife, from whom he was separated and who had earlier gone mad, and his daughter, of whom he had always been extremely fond, were relieved through subscriptions collected by his friend John Hall-Stevenson and by the posthumous publication, in 1769, of three more volumes of his sermons.

In 1769, a year after Laurence Sterne's death, the ubiquitous James Boswell (1740–95) had rooms in Old Bond Street during one of his many extended visits to London from Edinburgh, where he practised intermittently at the Bar. Also lodging in Old Bond Street at that time was the famous Corsican patriot Pasquale de Paoli, who looms very large in Boswell's "voluminous page". Boswell in fact moved his lodgings to Bond Street in order to dance attendance on Paoli, who had then only just arrived in London from Corsica. The enthusiastic Boswell, it seemed to some, made himself "foolishly conspicuous" in the

James Boswell, whose journal includes interesting recollections of his stay in Old Bond Street in 1769

General Pasquale de Paoli, Boswell's much admired neighbour in Old Bond Street

Dr Samuel Johnson, whose frequent visits to Bond Street were encouraged by Boswell's hospitality

Sir Thomas Lawrence, who established himself in Old Bond Street early in his rising career

40

attentions he paid to Paoli – Boswell ever loved a famous name. He was dubbed "Corsica Boswell" by the unimpressed.

General Pasquale de Paoli (1725–1807) had, in the very recent past, led his people in an heroic struggle against their oppressors, the Genoese, who subsequently, in 1768, sold the island to France. For a year Paoli had kept the French army at bay, but eventually he was overpowered. He escaped to England, where he was welcomed as a hero, not least by his fan Boswell, who had, a few years before, been introduced to the General in Corsica, finding him "a most extraordinary man. His abilities in politics and in war, his learning, his eloquence, and his generous sentiments render him truly illustrious."

For a time Boswell had whole-heartedly immersed himself in Coriscan affairs, preparing for publication *An Account of Corsica*. Ever on the make, he hoped that this would be a stepping-stone to friendship also with the statesmen of England. Indeed Lord Chatham, then living in Bond Street, whom Boswell called upon in Corsican dress at Grafton House, honoured him with a three-page letter in 1766, praising his enthusiasm. In the following year Boswell had the glorious effrontery to write to him: "Could your Lordship find time to honour me now and then with a letter? To correspond with a Paoli and with a Chatham is enough to keep a young man ever ardent in the pursuit of virtuous fame."

The *Account of Corsica* appeared in 1768 and *Essays in Favour of the Brave Corsicans* the following year: confident of resulting fame, Boswell now launched himself with gusto into London society, bragging of his high living and great company.

On September 21st he had news of Paoli's arrival in London, and the next day renewed his friendship: "I then went to Old Bond Street and called on Paoli," he writes in his journal. "A footman who opened the door said he was not well and could not see company, and made a great many difficulties. 'Stay,' said I. 'Get me a bit of paper and pen and ink, and I'll write a note to him.' His *valet de chambre* came down.

Seeing something about him like what I had been used to see in Corsica, I asked him in Italian if he was a Corsican. He answered, 'Yes, Sir.' 'Oh, then,' said I, 'there is no occasion to write. My name is Boswell.' No sooner had I said this than Giuseppe (for that was his name) gave a jump, catched hold of my hand and kissed it, and clapped his hands several times upon my shoulders with such a natural joy and fondness as flattered me exceedingly. Then he ran upstairs before me like an Italian harlequin, being a very little fellow, and, opening the door of the General's bedchamber, called out, 'Mr Boswell.' I heard the General give a shout before I saw him. When I entered he was in his night-gown and nightcap. He ran to me, took me all in his arms, and held me there for some time. I cannot describe my feelings on meeting him again. We sat down, and instantly were just as when we parted."

Invited to return for dinner, Boswell goes out for a while and walks down to St James's Street to "look at the company going to and coming from Court". Meeting the Duke of Queensberry in his sedan chair, he hurries him back to Paoli's lodgings and proudly introduces him.

Boswell comments interestingly on the General's Bond Street rooms: "Paoli's lodgings were in the house where the Duchess of Douglas had lived," he tells us. "They were the most magnificent, I suppose, to be hired in all London." Boswell dined there with his admired friend, hanging on his every word: "I was filled with admiration whenever the General spoke."

Very conscious of his new social dignity now that such a friend as Paoli was at hand, Boswell orders himself some fine new clothes – "a genteel, plain, slate-blue frock suit, and a full suit of a kind of purple cloth with rich gold buttons, and Mr Dilly supplied me with a silver-hilted sword" – and moves his lodgings to Bond Street. "Paoli said he was sorry he had not room for me in the house with himself," he writes. "I could have wished it. But I did my best, and immediately took very handsome lodgings within a few doors of his, at a M. Renaud's, an old Swiss, whose wife kept a milliner's shop. She was a well-behaved, obliging woman. The Bishop of Peterborough had been her lodger many years. Indeed the apartments were excellent. I had a large dining-room with three windows to Old Bond Street, a bedchamber, and a dressing room, both looking into Burlington Gardens. So that I saw a pretty large extent of green ground and stately trees in the very centre of the court end of town." It is a most interesting description of typical good rooms in Georgian Old Bond Street. "I paid for my apartments in Old Bond Street a guinea and a half a week," he writes, "only the half of what they bring in winter. I found there a pretty little Yorkshire maid called Mary. I determined however to get a servant who could speak Italian."

Boswell's journal is very detailed for the next couple of days as he haunts Paoli, though on that first day, Saturday September 23rd, he meets with little success: "I had called at the General's in the morning and he was not up," he tells us, "and when I called at night he was gone to bed." However, next morning he gains admittance, and again in the evening: "He had just gone to bed. But he desired that I would walk up. I was afraid to see him in bed, lest it might lessen his dignity and diminish my grand idea of him. But it had no such effect. Though his hands and arms were under the clothes and he showed his countenance only, he appeared with superior lustre. His eyes alone expressed the vivacity of his mind. He talked of the political heats of this country and of his own in certain situation with ease and cheerful manliness."

The following day Boswell records that he "dined at Paoli's. He had a good table, having dinner at a crown a head from the Brawn's Head Tavern in Bond Street." In the evening Boswell is back, introducing his friend Thomas Sheridan, the actor and elocutionist, to Paoli, and lingering afterwards to discuss in private his impending marriage, which is much on his mind at this time, and allowing Paoli to read that *"most valuable letter"* from his "dearest Peggy", which Paoli dashingly translates into Italian.

The meetings with Paoli continue, but Boswell's detailed journal breaks off here, though we do have a description of Boswell's much anticipated introduction of Samuel Johnson to Paoli in his *Life of Johnson*, for which great work Boswell had been assiduously gathering up notes since he first met Johnson in 1763. The *Life* contains a rich fund of information both about the eminent Doctor and the somewhat artless Boswell, unashamedly seeking out the presence of great men.

In October – probably the 31st and not the 10th as stated in the *Life* – Boswell brings Johnson to Bond Street to perform the important introduction to Paoli: "I had greatly wished that two men for whom I had the highest value should meet," writes Boswell. "They met with a manly ease, mutually conscious of their own abilities and the abilities one of each other. The General spoke Italian and Dr Johnson English, and understood one another very well with a little aid of interpretation from me, in which I compared myself to an isthmus which joins two great continents."

After the meeting with Paoli, Johnson returned with Boswell to his own Bond Street lodgings "and drank tea till late in the night. He said General Paoli had the loftiest port of any man he had ever seen."

Shortly after this meeting, a famous gathering of notables had assembled in Boswell's rooms: "He" – meaning Dr Johnson – Boswell writes in the *Life*, "honoured me with his company at dinner on the 16 of October at my lodgings in Old Bond Street, with Sir Joshua Reynolds, Mr Garrick, Dr Goldsmith, Mr Murphy, Mr Bickerstaff, and Mr Thomas Davies." Arthur Murphy and Isaac Bickerstaff were both playwrights well known in their day. Thomas Davies was an actor and bookseller, at whose shop Dr Johnson and Boswell had first been introduced. The engaging David Garrick, still considered to have been perhaps the most versatile actor in the whole history of the British stage, was a great contrast to the strange, brilliant little Irishman, Oliver Goldsmith, who, entirely without Garrick's good looks and charm, was less of a favourite of Boswell's – who saw him as a blundering fool, full of vanity and petty jealousies. Shortly before this gathering Boswell had recorded meeting Goldsmith for the first time in three years at Tom Davies' bookshop; they had dined together a few days later and it was on this occasion that Boswell had first met the great portrait painter, Sir Joshua Reynolds, then at the height of his career.

Boswell's account of his dinner party continues: "Garrick played round him [Dr Johnson] with a fond vivacity, taking hold of the breasts of his coat, and, looking up in his face with a lively archness, talking how well he now was; while the Sage, shaking his head, beheld him with a gentle complacency. One of the company was late in coming. I started the usual question upon such occasions if I should not order dinner to be served, and said, 'Ought six people to be kept waiting for one?' 'Why, yes,' answered Johnson, 'if the one will suffer more by your sitting down than the six will do by waiting.' There was a delicate humanity in this observation. Goldsmith, to divert the tedious minutes, strutted about bragging of his dress, and I believe was seriously vain of it, for his mind was wonderfully prone to that passion. 'Come, come,' said Garrick, 'talk no more of that. You are, perhaps, the worst – eh, eh!' Goldsmith was eagerly breaking in, when Garrick went on, laughing ironically, 'Nay, you will always *look* like a gentleman, but I am talking of being well or ill *dressed*.' 'Well, let me tell you,' said Goldsmith, 'when my tailor brought home my bloom-coloured coat, he said, "Sir, I have a favour to beg of you. When anybody asks you who made your clothes, say John Filby at the Harrow in Water Lane." ' Johnson. 'Why, Sir, that was because he knew the strange colour would attract crowds to gaze at it, and thus they might hear of him and see how well he might make a coat even of so absurd a colour.' "

Boswell proceeds to recount the ebb and flow of the dinner-time conversation, concerned mostly with literary subjects, and characterised most strongly by Johnson's booming pronouncements. At this time Samuel Johnson was already advanced in years and reputation as his century's great arbiter in the world of letters. Johnson no doubt enjoyed a forum such as Boswell's dinner party, though even his friends were inclined to admit that his manners on such occasions wanted refinement. According to Nathanial Wraxall "his rugged exterior and garb, his uncouth gestures, his convolutions and distortions, when added to the rude or dogmatical manner in which he delivered his opinions and decision on every point, rendered him so disagreeable in company, and so oppressive in conversation, that all the superiority of his talents could not make full amends, in my estimation, for these defects."

The less fastidious Boswell is, however, not offended by the "ox in a china-shop". He seems greatly to have enjoyed his eminent friend's antics and pronouncements, though he also had cause to feel the sharpness of his teeth. Sent back to his Bond Street rooms one evening with a flea in his ear, he admits that, "All the harsh observations which I had ever heard made upon his character, crowded into my mind; and I seemed to myself like the man who had put his head into the lion's mouth a great many times with perfect safety, but at last had it bit off."

In November of 1769 Boswell departed again for Scotland, no doubt leaving his Old Bond Street lodgings with pleasant memories. According to a report in *The Times* of April 26th, 1875, a painting by the Victorian artist W. P. Frith of "the interior of these lodgings, with portraits of the guests, a fancy scene . . . was sold at Messrs Christie & Manson's rooms, a few days before the above date, for upwards of £4,000 – a larger sum than ever was paid for the painting of an English artist during his lifetime."

At the time of the French Revolution, Pasquale de Paoli became Governor of Corsica, but, not satisfied with this status for his country, he organised an insurrection against the French, favouring union with England. In 1796 he was back in London.

Literature has not been the only of the arts represented among Bond Street's lodgers. The portrait and history painter James Northcote, R.A. (1746–1831), the pupil, assistant and biographer of Reynolds, lived at 2 Old Bond Street in 1781. Before settling in London he had spent three years in Rome, years which had stirred his love of history and which led to a series of "large, competent and dull canvases". He himself was, however, far from dull: he was a well-known "character" of his time, immortalised in Hazlitt's *Conversations with Northcote*.

Sir Thomas Lawrence, R.A. (1769–1830) moved from Jermyn Street to 24 Old Bond Street in 1791 and then crossed the road to number 29, where he stayed till 1794. In these years he was already a young man of great promise. The son of a Bristol innkeeper, he had, from the tender age of ten, been greatly admired for his precocious portraits; at twelve he had actually had his own early studio in Bath. He was largely self-taught, though at eighteen he had entered as a student of the Royal Academy. At twenty he was commissioned to paint his remarkable full-length portrait of Queen Charlotte, which brought him well-deserved renown. Having been strongly recommended by King George III, he was, in 1791, elected an Associate of the Royal Academy.

According to the diary of Lawrence's painter friend Joseph Farington, Lawrence paid two hundred guineas a year for his lodgings at 29 Old Bond Street, his charges for portraits being at that time between forty and one hundred and sixty guineas. Work was in abundance and his great industry was legendary: it was reported by D. E. Williams that "sometimes he would begin a head at ten in the morning, and finish it by four in the afternoon. Such exertions exhausted him, and he sought repose, not in conviviality, but in a change to milder occupations under his own roof, or sometimes in the *délassement* of an evening with a few private friends, who were selected with a taste that reflected credit on his discernment."

Though suspicious of the vapidity of fashionable society, Lawrence was nevertheless enough in it to make useful contacts which enabled him to meet his sitters on equal terms. In his early days in Bath he had drawn the portrait of the famous Georgiana, Duchess of Devonshire, who had been captivated by the precocious boy and later "always

47

noticed and invited him to Devonshire House" – which was, of course, very close to Bond Street. It was observed that "in such society, consisting of all the men and women of taste and refinement and wit and learning of the age, his manners could not fail to improve, and attain the peculiar grace and urbanity which marked them through life." Handsome and rapidly gaining poise, he enjoyed many social flirtations.

By August 1794 Lawrence, by now a full member of the Royal Academy, was sufficiently elevated in financial and social status to move from his Old Bond Street rooms to a house in Piccadilly, which faced Green Park. His rooms at number 24 Old Bond Street were later occupied by the young William Harrison Ainsworth; later still they became the Artists' Benevolent Institution. In later life Lawrence's success was to continue. In 1792 he was appointed principal portrait-painter in ordinary to the King. From there he went on to become the most famous portrait painter of his time.

Ozias Humphrey, R.A. (1742–1810), the miniature painter, lived at 13 Old Bond Street in 1796, at the end of his career and shortly before the final complete failure of his eyesight. In 1772 he had had an accident which affected his eyes so that in subsequent years he worked only for one brief period on miniatures: instead he turned to crayon drawing, a medium in which he was highly proficient and industrious, though he never succeeded in making his fortune either in London or in Europe and India, to which he travelled. When he returned home in 1788 his health and spirits were broken. He was, however, in 1791, elected to the Royal Academy, and later he was given the title of Portrait Painter in Crayons to His Majesty.

So much for the artists: there were also men of action. Right at the end of the eighteenth century, the renowned English soldier Sir Thomas Picton (1758–1815) lived at 146 New Bond Street between 1797 and 1800. His distinguished army career had, at the time of his lodging in Bond Street, led him to the heights of the governorship of

Trinidad and, subsequently, Tobago. In the dark hour of his career he was packed back to England to stand trial for allowing the use of torture on a woman prisoner, permitted under the old Spanish laws but frowned upon by England. Though found technically guilty, he was acquitted on appeal. In later years he served with distinction under Wellington in the Peninsular War, and was killed at Waterloo. His body was publicly displayed for a week at Edward Street, St Marylebone.

In the same house that the poet James Thomson had lived in the early part of the eighteenth century, 141 New Bond Street, on the site of the present 147, Horatio Nelson (1758–1805) spent painful months of recuperation in 1797, after losing his right arm.

After his great victory against the Spanish fleet off Cape St Vincent on February 14th, 1797, Nelson was sent to Teneriffe with a hopelessly inadequate squadron to capture a richly-laden Spanish ship. The attack, made on the night of July 21st, was repulsed and severe losses were suffered by the English: Nelson himself had his right elbow shattered by a bullet and his arm had to be amputated hastily and inexpertly while he was still on board his ship, the *Theseus*.

Deeply mortified by his failure and mutilation, Nelson wrote in a letter, bravely scrawled with his reluctant left hand: "A left-handed admiral will never again be considered as useful; therefore the sooner I get to a very humble cottage the better; and make room for a sounder man to serve the State."

However, it was to no "humble cottage" that he was consigned, but, after a few days in Bath, to the opulence of New Bond Street – which, regrettably, must have offered little comfort for he was feverish and weak. The ligature which had been applied to his wound on board the *Theseus* held fast to an artery and nerve so that he suffered intense pain from the burning, swollen stump of his arm. Robert Southey in his *Life of Nelson* describes his "long and painful" sufferings: "A nerve had been taken up in one of the ligatures at the time of the operation; and the ligature, according to the practice of the French surgeons, was of silk, instead of waxed thread: this produced a constant irritation and discharge; and the ends of the ligature being pulled every day, in hopes of bringing it away, occasioned fresh agony. He had scarcely any intermission of pain, day or night, for three months after his return to England. Lady Nelson, at his earnest request, attended the dressing of his arm, till she had acquired sufficient resolution and skill to dress it herself."

For Nelson's wife, Fanny, this period of his convalescence "at the lodgings of Mr Jones" was the last happy one she was to spend with him, before the ascendance of Lady Hamilton. The shortcomings of their marriage seem to have been temporarily overcome so that Nelson could actually write: "I found my domestic happiness perfect." They had moved to Bond Street so that Nelson could be examined by the foremost surgeons: William Cruikshank and Thomas Keate, surgeon to the Prince of Wales, both saw him and, rejecting the idea of another operation, recommended that poultices be applied to the wound. For the rest, time and quiet would, they hoped, eventually do their work.

The newspapers made much of the defeat at Teneriffe, though this did not diminish the heroic status of Nelson in the eyes of his people, and upon his return to London he was welcomed by all levels of society. His days of convalescence in Bond Street did not keep him in clinical isolation: he had frequent meetings with both friends and the important men of his day and, according to newspapers, was "daily at the Admiralty", anxiously keeping in touch with the progress of the war, fearing constantly that there would be further critical developments before he would be well enough to go to sea again.

Southey recounts a more light-hearted incident during this stay in London: "Not having been in England till now, since he lost his eye, he went to receive a year's pay as smart money; but could not obtain payment, because he had neglected to bring a certificate from a surgeon that the sight was actually destroyed. A little irritated that this

Lord Nelson spent painful days of recuperation in New Bond Street in 1797 after the loss of his arm, during which time sketches for this bronze by Lawrence Gahagan were made in his lodgings

Lady Hamilton, whose last debt-bedevilled years were, much later, eked out in a succession of temporary lodgings

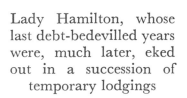

form should be insisted upon, because, though the fact was not apparent, he thought it was sufficiently notorious, he procured a certificate at the same time for the loss of his arm, saying they might just as well doubt one as the other. This put him in good humour with himself, and with the clerk who had offended him. On his return to the office, the clerk, finding it was only the annual pay of a captain, observed he thought it had been more. 'Oh!' replied Nelson, 'this is only for an eye. In a few days I shall come for an arm; and in a little time longer, God knows, most probably for a leg.' Accordingly, he soon afterwards went, and with perfect good humour exhibited the certificate of the loss of his arm."

The great event during his stay in London, however, was his investiture as a Knight of the Bath by George III. He also was given the Freedom of the City of London and the security of a pension of £1,000 a year.

Nelson, unlike Wellington, was a patient sitter for portraits and several of his best known likenesses were painted from sketches made during this period. In addition to paintings, Lawrence Gahagan showed a sculpture at the next Academy which was based on sketches made in the Bond Street rooms. Nelson's appearance at this time was as he was always to be remembered: in his best known portraits the pathos of his sightless right eye and empty right sleeve are completely overridden by the strong character and infectious high spirits which still shine out of his determined face.

In build he was very slight though his height of 5′ 5½″ was not particularly small for his day. One contemporary observer described him as "one of the most insignificant figures I ever saw . . . His weight cannot be more than seventy pounds"; but another added, "When induced to talk the things he knew he took on stature." Neither robust nor handsome, his strength and sense of presence was achieved by sheer personality. His manners were described as unaffectedly simple; he was not one to stand upon his dignity. Those who met him seemed frequently hardly to have noticed his physical shortcomings: they were left with the impression of an animated man of action whose boundless enthusiasm poured out in his vehement conversation.

During Nelson's stay in Bond Street, news reached London of Admiral Duncan's total destruction of the Dutch fleet at Camperdown on October 11th, 1797, and Southey has the following description: "One night, during this state of suffering, after a day of constant pain, Nelson retired early to bed, in hope of enjoying some respite by means of laudanum. He was at that time lodging in Bond Street; and the family were soon disturbed by a mob knocking loudly and violently at the door. The news of Duncan's victory had been made public, and the house was not illuminated. But when the mob were told that Admiral Nelson lay there in bed, badly wounded, the foremost of them made answer, 'You shall hear no more from us tonight': and, in fact, the feeling of respect and sympathy was communicated from one to another with such effect, that, under the confusion of such a night, the house was not molested again."

Nelson was of course greatly satisfied at the news of Duncan's victory, though, he confessed, "I would give this other arm to be with Duncan at this moment."

On the morning of December 4th Nelson awoke to find that the pain had suddenly ceased. Southey writes: "the surgeon was immediately sent for to examine it; and the ligature came away with the slightest touch. From that time it began to heal. As soon as he thought his health established, he sent the following form of thanksgiving to the minister of St George's, Hanover Square: 'An officer desires to return thanks to Almighty God for his perfect recovery from a severe wound, and also for the many mercies bestowed on him.'"

Nelson also lost no time in conveying his good news to the Admiralty, and indeed the Earl of St Vincent was equally impatient for Nelson to be back in command. In March 1798, after a sojourn at a new address, 96, later 103, New Bond Street – the only original residence of Nelson now remaining here – he hoisted his flag on the *Vanguard* and was sent into the Mediterranean with a small squadron to watch the French; not long afterwards he won his remarkable victory at Aboukir Bay. He returned an even greater hero: the Queen welcomed him with ardour and Lady Hamilton, whose acquaintance had meanwhile been renewed to great effect, with rapture.

By January 1801 Nelson was no longer at Bond Street, for his solicitor records the final rupture between the famous admiral and his wife, not far away on the other side of Piccadilly. "I was breakfasting with Lord and Lady Nelson, at their lodgings in Arlington Street, when Lord Nelson spoke of something which had been done or said by 'dear Lady Hamilton'; upon which Lady Nelson rose from her chair, and exclaimed with much vehemence, 'I am sick of hearing of dear Lady Hamilton, and am resolved that you shall give up either her or me.' Lord Nelson, with perfect calmness, said: 'Take care, Fanny, what you say. I love you sincerely; but I cannot forget my obligations to Lady Hamilton, or speak of her otherwise than with affection and admiration.'" Lady Nelson left the house, and they never lived together again.

Lady Emma Hamilton (*c.* 1761–1815) herself lived in New Bond Street, but only several years after Nelson's death and shortly before she was arrested and imprisoned for debt, to be bailed out, a year later, by Alderman Joshua Smith, who pitied her sad and lonely condition, and helped her to escape to Calais, where she died in 1815, poor, fat and forgotten.

When still in the full bloom of unwasted youth (she had already had an unusually colourful career and two children), "a woman of extreme beauty, winning manners and shady antecedents", she had married Sir William Hamilton in 1791. It was in 1798, after Nelson's residence in New Bond Street, that their immortal relationship first blossomed, and their daughter, "our loved Horatia", was born in London at the beginning of 1801.

Both Sir William Hamilton, who died in 1803, and Nelson, who died two years later, left her very large amounts of money, but evidently not enough to keep up with debts she incurred, probably partly through gambling, and certainly through wasteful expenditure, and the hopeless mismanagement of her affairs. Within three years of the death of Nelson she was already in almost helpless difficulties. Her admirer "Old Q", the 4th Duke of Queensberry, who died in 1810, also left her an annuity of £500, but so much complicated litigation was needed to unravel his enormous estate that Emma never received a penny of it.

On September 4th, 1811, during the first of her sojourns in Bond Street, she made her will, a "curious essay in rigmarole": "I Emma Hamilton of No. 150 Bond Street London Widow of the Right Honourable Sir William Hamilton formerly Minister at the Court of Naples being in sound mind and body do give to my dearly beloved Horatia Nelson dau\(^r\) of the great and glorious Nelson all that I shall be possessed of at my death money jewells pictures wine furniture books wearing apparel silver gold-plated or silver-gilt utensils of every sort I may have in my house or houses or of any other persons' houses at my death any marbles bronzes busts plaster of Paris or in short every thing that belonged to me I give to my best beloved Horatia Nelson all my table linen laces ornaments in short everything that I have I give to her any money either in the house or at my bankers all debts that may be owing to me I beg that she may have I give to Horatia Nelson all silver with inscription with Viscount Nelson's name or his arms I give to her wou'd to God it was more for her sake . . ." She was, unfortunately, over-optimistic. By the time of her death it was to be very, very much less. She goes on to entrust Horatia to the generosity of the Prince Regent who, she points out, had failed to remunerate *her* as he "often promised" for "the services that I have rendered to my King and Country and as I have never been remunerated nor ever received one sixpence . . ."

The catalogue of possessions was soon to be drastically reduced.

During the last unhappy and tortuous years of her life, misfortune was heaped upon misfortune. Everywhere cheated by strangers and deserted by friends, she moved from lodging to lodging in Piccadilly – from Bond Street to Albemarle Street to Dover Street and back again to Bond Street, keeping her little household together by fresh borrowings. With her she had Horatia, a female companion and Dame Francis, an old servant; and sometimes Mr Russell, employed to write petitions on her behalf. After each removal she would rearrange her few remaining bits of furniture and little collection of articles of sentimental association which sang of a better past – a bust of Nelson, portraits of Nelson and Sir William, a collection of decorations, a gold box with the freedom of Oxford, a prized dinner service . . .

Amidst the remnants of her life she prepared to petition the Prince Regent, and even the mad old King himself. Early in 1813 the Prince actually dined with her in her Bond Street rooms and must have rekindled hopes of assistance from above. These, however, were dashed when, early the following year, some of Nelson's letters to her were published in which he disparaged the Prince as a frequenter of pimps and bawds. If the Prince had ever meant to help her, he clearly would not do so now.

Drink and religion were her two sources of consolation during these dreary days; mostly drink. She dwelt miserably on the past and quarrelled constantly with her child. During the stress of the Bond Street days she complained in the following extraordinary terms to the twelve-year-old Horatia: "I grieve and lament to see the increasing strength of your turbulent passions. I weep and pray you may not be totally lost, my fervent prayers are offered up to God for you. I hope you may become yet sensible of your eternal welfare. I shall go join your father and my blessed mother and may you on your death bed have as little to reproach yourself as your affectionate mother has, for I can glorify and say I was a good child. *Can Horatia Nelson say so – I am unhappy to say you cannot.* No answer to this. I shall tomorrow look out for a school for your sake to *save you*, that you may bless the memory of an injured mother. P.S. Look on me as gone from this world."

It is difficult to believe that the spirited Emma had herself been anything of a model child. Anyway, despite the letter, Horatia remained with her "injured mother" till the end, and later mended her ways sufficiently to be the wife of a clergyman. She died in 1881.

In June 1813 Lady Hamilton's affairs had come to so desperate a pass that Alderman Smith bought goods and chattels from her to the value of £490, while in July an auction of her effects was held, disposing of furniture, books, pictures, the box, the Order of the Star and the treasured dinner service; even the goose-feather bed bought by Nelson. Her arrest for debt soon followed, with her last lonely months of survival in France after her escape from prison. It was a poor end to a rich life.

At 148 New Bond Street the half-mad duellist Lord Camelford had lodgings around the turn of the century, which he is said to have preferred to his magnificent mansion, Camelford House. Thomas Pitt, second Baron Camelford (1775–1804) had, earlier in his fiery career, entered the navy. Put ashore for insubordination at Hawaii in 1794, he had had to work his passage home, afterwards ineffectually challenging his commander George Vancouver to a duel. In 1798 he shot Charles Peterson, the first lieutenant of the *Perdrix*, during a dispute concerning seniority, but was acquitted by court-martial. The same year his now tarnished name was struck off the list of commanders at his own request in consequence of an altercation with the Admiralty. He now began to achieve his extraordinary notoriety for disorderly conduct: he was soon known throughout London for the alacrity with which he provoked quarrels, frequently with perfect strangers, and for his deadliness in the field. Many stories circulated about his colourful encounters.

In October 1797, when all the West End was gladly illuminated to celebrate the victory at Camperdown – and the crowd politely allowed

A scene from *Tom Jones* in which Squire Western is surprised to discover his daughter with Tom in his Bond Street lodgings

the house in which Nelson lay to be an exception – neither his friends nor landlord could induce the pugnacious Camelford to permit a candle to be set in his windows. The enraged patriotic mob began to attack the house, stoning the windows. Camelford was fortunately prevented by a friend from rushing at the crowd with his pistol: but, armed instead with a stout cudgel, he charged outside to meet them and began laying about him violently until eventually he was overpowered by many hands and rolled over and over in the gutter. For once crestfallen and slightly injured, he beat an indignant retreat indoors while the mob smashed the lower windows of the house.

On another occasion, two friends of Camelford's, James and Horace Smith, who had witnessed one of his quarrels in a theatre the night before, called at his lodgings in Bond Street in February 1804 to offer evidence, if it were needed, that he had been assaulted. Their motive might have been questionable, but they left an interesting description of what they saw in his lodgings: "Over the fire-place in the drawing-room . . . were ornaments strongly expressive of the pugnacity of the peer. A long, thick bludgeon lay horizontally supported by two brass hooks. Above this was placed parallel one of lesser dimensions, until a pyramid of weapons gradually arose, tapering to a horsewhip."

A fortnight later, however, Camelford picked his last quarrel. On March 6th he swaggered into a coffee house to insult his former friend Mr Best, whose ex-mistress had reported to Camelford some disparaging remarks supposedly made about him by Best. It seems that she backed the wrong horse. The two agreed to meet next morning "in the fields behind Holland House". Camelford fired first, but missed. When Best returned fire he fell dangerously wounded, and died three days later.

Renowned frequenters of Bond Street, as opposed to actual residents, are too numerous to mention, though an exception may perhaps be made for three of them. One amusing anecdote tells of a wager which Charles James Fox made with George, Prince of Wales (afterwards

59

George IV) as to who would see the larger number of cats on his side of Bond Street. Knowing that cats love sunshine, Fox chose the sunny side of the street and counted thirteen, while the Prince, on the shady side, saw none.

The fine old General Oglethorpe, who died in 1785, at the age of eighty-nine, was a frequenter of Bond Street, and, in his early life, of the Conduit Mead, years before New Bond Street was built. It is said that he had often shot woodcocks over these fields – and certainly he was known in his day as the best shot of birds on the wing.

Real people aside, Bond Street also made one appearance in the fiction of the eighteenth century which is of particular interest, and which reflects the fashionableness of the street as a place for lodgings. A considerable portion of the action in the later part of Fielding's *Tom Jones*, published in 1749, takes place in Bond Street (whether Old or New we cannot tell), described as "a very good part of town". Mrs Miller was "the widow of a clergyman, and was left by him at his decease in possession of two daughters and of a complete set of manuscript sermons." Squire Allworthy helped her very generously in her distress, setting her up as a lodging-house keeper in Bond Street, and when in London he went to lodge with her. Tom Jones, not knowing this, was led by circumstances to the same house, where he too lodges and finds in the landlady a very good friend. Fielding also introduces Bond Street in his *Amelia* (1752), where, on foot, Booth attends Colonel Bath in his sedan chair to the house of an eminent surgeon so that his wounds may be dressed.

The whole of Mayfair had, by the middle of the eighteenth century, become an area of increasing prestige, and it was developing quickly. Bond Street with its fine shops had by this time become *the* region of fashion, which, in the words of Pennant, "abounded with shopkeepers of both sexes of superior taste", supplying all the needs and wants of a rich neighbourhood with only the best of merchandise.

Many of the early shops and their wares sound quaint to the modern ear, though services provided were perhaps only slight variations of modern counterparts. Already at the end of the seventeenth century there was established at "Mr Trout's in Bond Street, near Piccadilly, the second House of the left-hand side" a "beauty doctor" who loudly proclaims her merits on her trade bill: "Let every one then consider that such a Person as this Lady is, is a PEARL AND A TREASURE, for she works almost Night and Day for the good of mankind, which a great many persons of the first rank can testify." Among her mysteries she offered "Balsamick Essence, with several other incomparable Cosmeticks", the use of which would make happy customers "pleasing to their Husbands . . . that they might not be offended at their deformities and turn to others." The use of make-up by the ladies of polite society was to develop into a fine art during the eighteenth century, the toilet-table of a lady of fashion being described as a complete chemical laboratory. There were hidden dangers, however: of one of the beautiful Gunnings, it was said that her end was accelerated by the use of cosmetics with a dangerously high content of white lead.

In the early days of New Bond Street, a perfumery shop was opened by James Smyth somewhere between Grosvenor Street and Brook Street, selling lavender water, perfumed powder, soap, wash-balls and pomatum, while not far off the confectioner Richard Robinson offered pistachio nuts, prunellos, comfits, aniseed, limes and flowered jelly glasses.

One of the earliest inhabitants of New Bond Street was Austin, the famous pieman, a disciple of Braund, the great cook. In the *Memoirs of the Bedford Coffee House* (1763) there is a reference to a duel at the Braund's Head in Bond Street, and James Boswell, while lodging nearby, enjoyed dinners "at a crown a head from the Brawn's Head Tavern in Bond Street". This name seems to have been corrupted into Brown, in which form it is found in an amusing article on street signs in the *Universal Spectator* of January 8th, 1743: "Some hang up their own heads for a sign," it is stated here, "as did Lebeck and Brown, to

"Sandwich Carrots! Dainty Sandwich Carrots!" – an old cry in
New Bond Street attracting some attention in a delightful
cartoon by James Gillray dated 1796

show that they, in their art of Cookery, were as great men as your Eugenes and Marlboroughs in the art of War."

By the end of the eighteenth century a great number of shops were already established in Bond Street, supplying a marvellous range of merchandise. They were becoming increasingly elegant, many displaying the Royal Warrant. There were book and music publishers, tailors, milliners, boot- and shoe-makers, furriers, an umbrella- and parasol-maker, woollen and linen drapers, gold and silver lacemen, jewellers, perfumers, chemists and druggists, tobacconists, carriage manufacturers and livery stables, a saddler and harness-maker, a gun-maker, carpet manufacturers, cabinet-makers and upholsterers, lamp-makers, glass, porcelain and china shops, a seedsman and florist, butchers, poulterers, fishmongers, cheesemongers, grocers, pastrycooks and bakers, dairies, fruiterers, tea and coffee and wine and spirit merchants and a "fish sauce warehouse".

Up till 1762 it was usual for each establishment to have its own special sign hanging over its bow window as a means of ostentatious advertisement. There were Turk's Heads and Plumes of Feathers and Civit Cats, all in some obvious or vague manner connected to the shopkeeper's class of business. A New Bond Street mercer traded under the sign of the Coventry Cross, as it was in that city that silk ribbons were manufactured. Such signs, a useful early substitute for street numbering, began to increase and increase in size as shopkeepers attempted to outdo their neighbours in self-advertisement until they were a forest of metalwork darkening the street and creating a hazard from above on a gusty day. In 1762 a law was passed forbidding all such signs, and instead of Olive Trees and Flaming Swords, Bond Street was given street numbers, Old and New Bond Street being separately numbered.

By the mid eighteenth century Bond Street had become a fashionable promenade in which it was essential for every woman of class to be seen. Ladies of high fashion found ideal stages on which to display their beauty (real or supposed) and latest clothes in the large and elegant shops of London, of which the finest were to be found in Bond Street, in the same way that the Frenchwoman shone from her box at the opera. Shopping was, already in the eighteenth century, a great preoccupation in the life of a London lady. In other countries this fascinating pastime did not manifest itself until much later as the appearance of large fashionable shops like those of Georgian Bond Street were much slower to appear even in France and Germany.

Wilhelm Bornemann, a contemporary, wrote of eighteenth-century Bond Street: "Here elegant ladies appear in different costumes for every hour of the day, changing them as simple folk do for the different seasons, displaying the latest creation of the restless world of fashion, buying and paying for everything twice and three times as much as would be charged in other parts of London. Everything must be bought in the shops of this renowned street if it is to find favour with refined taste."

Old and New Bond Street were a paradise for the fashionable shopper; here the elegant world would take its daily stroll, an activity which usually began at about four o'clock in the afternoon. Clever shopkeepers added a certain piquancy to the pleasures of the female shopper by employing dashingly handsome and dapper young men to attend their customers; the more attractive the company, the more eager were the shoppers.

The delights of Georgian Bond Street were, however, at least as much for male as for female shoppers. These were days when men dressed with an eye for colour, finery and delicacy equal to that of the most fastidious woman. In curling periwigs, bright embroidered coats and waistcoats and with finely bejewelled fingers, they too would drink deep of the fashionable pleasures of Bond Street.

Early on in the history of the street we are introduced to a special class of persons of wealth and leisure, the "Bond Street loungers", and the late eighteenth century was the time of the "Bond Street Roll". "A young fellow is nothing without the Bond Street Roll," declared a

"High Change in Bond Street" – a fashion caricature of 1796

"Bond Street Brilliants" outside Long's Hotel in late Georgian days

character in a play of the period. "A toothpick between his teeth and his knuckles crammed into his coat pocket, then away you go lounging lazily along."

In 1805 Pennant remarked that, if its builder had been able to foresee the extreme fashion in reserve for Bond Street, he would have made it wider. "But this," he muses, "is a fortunate circumstance for the Bond Street loungers, who thus get a nearer glimpse of the fashionable and generally titled ladies that pass and repass from two to five o' clock."

The Bond Street loungers set the fashion, determined what was done and not done, what was to be worn, and how, and when, popularised the cut of a coat, the hang of a sleeve, the placing of buttons. The signal for what was right came from Bond Street: those elsewhere who wanted to be smart had to shape their ways on the Bond Street lead.

In addition to a fine assortment of shops, Bond Street's fashionable eighteenth-century shoppers were also treated to some astonishing exhibitions. Bond Street loungers were invited to step in to see the "authentic sword" and a lock of hair of Julius Caesar, the "incontestable" mummy of Cleopatra and a necklace worn by "the late" Queen of Sheba.

Of more particular interest, however, is the advertisement in the *Morning Chronicle* of March 18th, 1799: "The real embalmed head of the powerful and renowned usurper, Oliver Cromwell, with the original dies for the medals struck in honour of his victory at Dunbar," it tells us, "are now exhibited at No. 5, in Mead Court, Old Bond Street (where the rattlesnake was shown last year); a genuine narrative relating to the acquisition, concealment, and preservation of these articles to be had at the place of exhibition."

Cromwell's head, it appears, was exhibited here by a man named Cox who kept a museum of curiosities, and who had purchased it from one of the Russell family, in whose hands it had been for a century. When Cox parted with his museum, he sold the head to three indi-

The flamboyant men's fashions of 1787 as popularised by a resplendent generation of
Bond Street Loungers

viduals who all in their turn met with sudden deaths, and the head became the property of the daughters or nieces of the last survivor. Nervous of so gruesome and unlucky a relic, they sold it to a medical man named Wilkinson, who preserved it in a special mahogany casket. The embalmed head was, according to a late-nineteenth-century report "not a mere skull but possesses flesh and a portion of the tongue and has a tooth still".

Despite the typically spurious ring about the Bond Street exhibition advertisement, the claims of authenticity for the head cannot easily be discounted. After the Restoration, the body of Oliver Cromwell had been exhumed and hanged for past treachery at Tyburn. There the body was buried, but the head was later displayed on top of Westminster Hall for many years, eventually being blown down and removed by a sentry. How even an embalmed head could have withstood the elements so long is not certain, but it is interesting that the Cambridge scientists who subjected it to careful examination in the 1930s agreed that the claims for it were quite possible. The size and age of the man from which it came, the moustache and small beard, the evidence of decapitation and the small depression in the skull above the left eye where Cromwell is known to have had one of his famous warts all made its authenticity possible, and the embalming techniques used were certainly those of the period in question. In 1960 the head was buried at Sydney Sussex College in Cambridge (Cromwell's own college), the exact locality of its last resting place being kept a close secret.

Cromwell's head

68

Chapter Three

LATTER DAYS

*   *   *

The days of the Regency were palmy days for Bond Street: fashion was king and Bond Street was his palace; it was here that every dandy in London had to be seen. In his satirical poem, "The Siamese Twins" (1831) Lord Lytton summed up all the infinite variety of excitements that Bond Street, in the years of George IV as Regent and King, could offer:

> And now our Brothers Bond Street enter,
> Dear Street, of London's charms the centre,
> Dear Street! where at a certain hour
> Man's follies bud forth into flower!
> Where the gay minor sighs for fashion:
> Where majors live that minors cash on;
> Where each who wills may suit his wish,
> Here choose a Guido – there his fish.

Looming largest of all in the fashionable society of the Regency was the remarkable Beau Brummell (1778–1840), who haunted Bond Street. So great was his social power at his height that Byron had declared he "would rather be Brummel than Bonaparte!" Having risen up the social ladder, from relatively humble beginnings, via Eton and a cornetcy in the Prince's own regiment, to become the undisputed arbiter of elegance in a competitively fashionable society, he had been aided only by a dauntless combination of impertinence, sarcasm and

Beau Brummell, haunter of Bond Street and arbiter of Regency elegance, who popularised full-length trousers and the typical small-waisted and high-collared coat shown here

natural grace. "His maxims on dress were excellent," conceded Hariette Wilson. "He possessed also, a sort of quaint dry humour, not amounting to anything like wit; but his affected manners and little absurdities amused for the moment. Then it became the fashion to court Brummell's society, which was enough to make many seek it, who cared not for it; and many more wished to be well with him through fear, for all knew him to be cold, heartless and satirical."

His position was assured by his friendship with the Prince Regent, who so sorely craved his approbation that he is said, on one occasion, to have started "to blubber when told that Brummell did not like the cut of his coat!"

A creator rather than a follower of fashion, Beau Brummell changed prevailing styles to suit himself, dressing with studied moderation in clothes of the utmost and most expensive simplicity. Roger Bouted de Monvel in *Beau Brummell and His Times* (1908) describes his customary appearance: "he wore his hair short without powder, shunned staring colours, and eventually chose a style of dress to which he always clung. He was invariably to be seen in a blue coat, a buff-coloured waistcoat, and either lace boots or light pumps, according as he was going for a walk or to a ball. His trousers were black, closely fitting, and buttoned above the ankle. His charming bearing and perfect figure were his chief attractions."

The reputation of Weston, Beau Brummell's tailor in Old Bond Street, was made by his client's great fame, and all the beautiful shops of Bond Street were prepared to offer handsome credit for the pleasure of Brummell's valued custom. In return, the wealth which came the way of Bond Street's outfitters through the influence of Brummell must have been immeasurable. To the fashionable dandies who were his followers expense was of no account. To ask, let alone argue, the price of anything was beneath the dignity of a gentleman, while practising economy or even living within one's means was only for the masses.

71

Over-confident of his own assured position, his head thick with his supposed wit, Beau Brummell eventually quarrelled with the Prince, making insulting and loud remarks about his figure. Loss of his royal follower, and gambling debts, brought him low: he retired to France, attempted to re-establish himself in Calais, and eventually died in a lunatic asylum in Caen in 1840.

The world of Beau Brummell and the Regency dandies was essentially a man's world, and Bond Street at this time was a man's street. Its "sporting" hotels and clubs were frequented exclusively by men; its shops sold mostly men's clothes: an increasing number of hatters and tailors and shirtmakers arose. The Bond Street loungers who put in their appearance every afternoon as they had for the past century now studied only each other: the ladies of fashion could only decently be seen before midday, and then carefully chaperoned by a servant.

During this period shopping facilities continued to develop on an increasingly grandiose scale. On the eastern side of the street in about 1820 a short-lived but splendid bazaar, the Western Exchange, was opened, consisting of one very large room, well furnished with a variety of stalls. It had an entrance in the rear into the Burlington Arcade. The Burlington Arcade itself was constructed in 1818 by Samuel Ware. This long covered passage lined with elegant shops then, as now, provided an "undulation conducive to the leisurely and agreeable spending of money". The contemporary illustration of the arcade shows the wall, with trees behind it, to the west of the entrance in Piccadilly, which indicates the gardens on the eastern side of Bond Street (which James Boswell so pleasantly overlooked from his lodgings). It was said that the inhabitants of Burlington House were much annoyed by the oyster-shells and other rubbish which were frequently thrown over the walls of the Bond Street gardens into the precincts of the great house. In 1815 Burlington House had been sold for £75,000 by the Duke of Devonshire to his uncle, Lord George Cavendish, who made great alterations to the interior and converted the riding-house

The Western Exchange *c.* 1820, an early Bond Street experiment in luxurious shopping

The Burlington Arcade, 1819, with a glimpse of the gardens behind Old Bond Street

and stables into a dwelling-house, building other stables behind the east side of the colonnade. The chief change, however, was the building of the Burlington Arcade on ground at the west side of the estate.

The laying out of Regent Street between 1813 and 1820 by Nash was calculated to alleviate what by then had become an intolerable congestion of traffic in Bond Street. The development of the Marylebone Park estate brought the West End's traffic problems to a head and necessitated some new means of communication with the west and north-west quarters of London. Before the building of Regent Street, the only convenient route from Pall Mall and Charing Cross to St Marylebone was by way of Bond Street, which, because here were concentrated all the best shops, would in any case have been thronged with pedestrians and carriages clattering along its cobbled road. One of the first objections to the proposed new Regent Street came from the vestrymen of St James's parish, who feared that the shopkeepers of Bond Street, Piccadilly and St James's Street would suffer if trade were drawn away to a new fashionable shopping street. Such fears, however, proved groundless: Bond Street never for a moment lost its pre-eminence as the most exclusive shopping district, or the important patronage of the Prince and Beau Brummell.

During the first half of the nineteenth century, Bond Street became famous as the headquarters of circulating libraries and booksellers, whose business included the selling of theatre tickets, while some were also publishers. Such circulating libraries were common until the middle of the century and these shops served as meeting places for young men about town with literary and theatrical interests.

One famous old bookshop with an unbroken history of over two hundred years used to stand at 29 New Bond Street. Opened by John Brindley in 1728, it was one of the original buildings in the street. Its old projecting doorway with two side-windows facing up and down the street was for long a familiar landmark. Brindley, also a publisher and printer, became famous for his beautiful bindings. Holding the Royal

Warrant, he traded under the sign of the King's Arms, and dedicated the first book he published to Queen Caroline – it being *Observations on the Small Pox*. Brindley's books were mostly learned, though he did issue some in lighter vein which might have attracted the attention of the fashionable ladies who paraded up and down Bond Street. It was probably Fielding's *Tom Jones* which did more to immortalise him than any other. He also published Dr Johnson's great Dictionary: "Thank God I have done with him," he is said to have sighed when presented with the last of the manuscript copy.

When Brindley died in 1758 his widow Penelope defied the social rules of the day and, with commendable spirit, herself continued the business for a year. She then died and James Robson, a former apprentice of Brindley, took over, running the business for nearly half a century, from 1759 to 1806. In addition to many more illustrious authors, he published a little volume entitled *The Elements of Clock and Watch Work* by Alexander Cumming, who for many years carried on a watchmaking business in Bond Street, displaying such scientific attainments that he was elected a Fellow of the Royal Society. Under Robson the bookshop at 29 New Bond Street became a great resort for the sociable intelligentsia of his day. Besides publishing and bookselling, Robson entered the proprietary chapel business, buying and restoring Trinity Chapel in Conduit Street, and drawing in, no doubt to good financial as well as spiritual effect, the wealthy crowds each Sunday to hear the admired sermons of Dr Beamish.

Between 1806 and 1830 the shop was in the hands of John Nornaville and William Fell. Less interested in publishing than rare books, Nornaville was a familiar figure in the sales rooms of his day, while his partner Fell had the advantage, through having been Robson's assistant, of being familiar to old clients, including Mrs Piozzi, whose patronage of the shop must have extended over nearly half a century.

Later in the nineteenth century, between 1830 and 1872, the brothers Thomas and William Boone took over, William retiring in favour of his

75

James Robson and Frederick Startridge Ellis, renowned eighteenth- and nineteenth-century owners of what was London's oldest bookshop

The interior of the old bookshop at 29 New Bond Street

nephew in 1860, while in 1872 and until 1885 it was owned by Frederick Startridge Ellis, under whose guidance it became to the *literati* of the nineteenth century very much what it had been to those of the eighteenth century under Robson. It is said that Tennyson, attired in his habitually sombre dress, would come in to pass a pleasant hour chatting with Ellis and examining his stock. Another frequent visitor was Gladstone who, even in the busiest years of his political career, found a little time to relax in browsing round the shelves of the old shop.

Finally continued by J. J. Holdsworth and George Smith, the fine old shop, a venerable institution in Mayfair, sadly disappeared in the 1930s.

Hookham, the friend of Shelley and Thomas Love Peacock, ran another well-known bookshop at 15 Old Bond Street which is mentioned in Hannah More's *Florio* (1786):

> For he to keep him from the vapours,
> Subscrib'd at Hookham's, saw the papers.

Hookham's Library was one of the most fashionable "lounges" in Bond Street at this time, where books could be borrowed as well as bought, and newspapers, then not yet ubiquitous, could be read. There men could relax as in the sabbatical atmosphere of a club, and meet others whom it was worth meeting. The Library is also mentioned in George Coleman's *Broad Grins* (1802):

> For novels should their critick hints succeed,
> The Muses might fare better when they took 'em:
> But it would fare extremely ill indeed
> With gentle Mr Lane and Messieurs Hookham.

It was in 1804 that Thomas Love Peacock first appeared before the public as an author, and it was Edward Hookham who first published his work.

John Ebers' bookshop was at 27 Old Bond Street, but his interest in booking opera boxes induced him to forsake his books and undertake the management of His Majesty's Theatre, which he continued from 1820 till 1827. He gave up a profitable business, but failed as a manager, losing, according to John Timbs, £44,080 in seven years. His son-in-law, William Harrison Ainsworth, later a successful novelist, took over his publishing business for a time. In a letter dated November 25th, 1826, Ainsworth wrote: "My shop is nearly ready. The partition has been erected and the library books removed, and my stock is being transferred to the vacant shelves. The customers stare and marvel at the change, but it has by no means a bad effect. My shop consists of a long, lobby-like room, terminating in a snug room, the shelves of which are loaded with goodly tomes, and the tables covered with magazines, newspapers, and new publications. When it is entirely completed it will have a very knowing appearance."

The novelist soon tired of the publishing business, however, and turned to writing. The business was taken over by other members of the family under the name of J. Ebers & Company.

Another famous theatrical agent was John Mitchell, who early in life was employed by William Sams, the instigator of the modern system of theatrical agency. In 1834 he opened a library at 33 Old Bond Street (at the corner of Stafford Street), and this was the headquarters of his exclusive business for forty years. In 1836 he established the Lyceum Theatre for Italian comic opera, and in 1842 brought over French plays and players to St James's Theatre. He died on December 11th, 1874, in his sixty-eighth year.

Mitchell's was a rendezvous of fashionable men, who went there to pick up the news of the day. Captain Gronow, in his *Reminiscences*, gives a curious anecdote of an eccentric baronet who was boasting there of his munificence, when in came a colonel of the Guards, who said, "My dear – –, I have just left our poor friend, Jack L, in a spunging-house, without a shilling in his pocket to pay for a mutton chop." "Is it possible?" asked the "charitable" baronet. "I will go and order some-

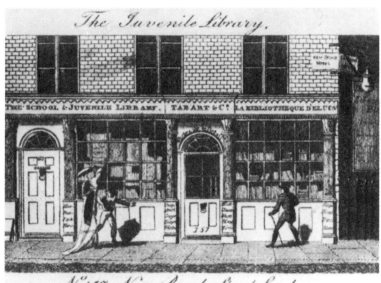

One of Bond Street's less renowned "libraries", catering for the needs of the younger generation

New Bond Street c.1835, from a drawing by T. C. Dibdin

79

thing which will make his heart glad." Jumping into his cab, he drove to the spunging-house, but, instead of giving his friend money, bought him a pottle of strawberries – which, he boasted, cost him two sovereigns!

In the nineteenth century, Bond Street was noted for its hotels. The Clarendon Hotel, built on the site of part of the gardens of Clarendon or Albemarle House, was in its day the biggest hotel in London, extending right back to Albemarle Street. Demolished in 1874, it used to be number 169 New Bond Street: the site was filled with a row of shops at the point where Cartier's at 160 now stands. The carriage entrance at the back was at 20 Albemarle Street, next to the Royal Institution, and it usefully avoided the congestion of traffic in Bond Street.

Opened by Jacquier, the French chef who was once in the service of Louis XVIII, while in exile at Hartwell House, the hotel had the reputation of being the only one in London where genuine French cooking could be enjoyed. The prices were on a level with its high repute. According to Captain Gronow, in 1814 "you could be sure of getting a genuine French dinner, never costing less than £3 or £4 a head, with a good bottle of claret or champagne at a guinea."

The hotel contained large suites of apartments where royal and noble personages could be put up in style during visits **to** London, and it was a favourite resort of dining clubs. Official banquets were often held here in the early nineteenth century, and also the meetings of the Association of Baronets "instituted", Edward Walford tells us in *Old and New London* (1897), "by the late amiable visionary, Sir Richard Broun, for the purpose of asserting the right of members of that order to the use of heraldic supporters, a coronet, the prefix of 'honourable', and other more tangible and substantial advantages." More importantly, the illustrious Club, founded by Sir Joshua Reynolds, whose famous members included Dr Johnson, perhaps the most exclusive club in the world, celebrated its centenary here on June 7th, 1864, when twenty-three members attended a special dinner.

In the 1870s there were difficulties over the renewal of the lease of the Clarendon Hotel, leading to its closure in 1872 and its demolition two years later.

Number 15, later renumbered 16, New Bond Street, on the southern corner of Clifford Street, used to be Long's Hotel, enlarged and rebuilt in 1888. Long's Hotel and Steven's Hotel in Bond Street, together with Limmer's at the corner of St George's Street and Conduit Street and Hatchett's in Piccadilly, were known as the "sporting" hotels of Mayfair, frequented largely by sportsmen and country squires or army officers. Exclusively men's hotels, only in the last few years of their existence did one or two women ever darken their doors.

The large, four-storeyed house which was the original Long's Hotel survived longest. Its smoking-room, to the right of the entrance, was a favourite meeting place for young men about town – Regency "dandies and country bachelors"; its cooking was apparently unpretentious but excellent: devilled soles were a speciality, while its whisky and soda was said to have been the best in town.

It was at Long's that Sir Walter Scott (1771–1832) and Lord Byron (1788–1824) met for the last time in September 1815. The brief, ill-sorted but sincere friendship between these two outstanding literary figures of their age, the fathers of the romantic movement, whose only other obvious point of similarity was a game leg, began only months before, in the spring of 1815, when the two met for the first time in the famous drawing-room at the offices of the publisher John Murray at 50 Albemarle Street, after the publication of *Childe Harold*. John Murray, then the most influential publisher in London, who had published the work of both Scott and Byron, used his drawing-room as the meeting place for all the distinguished men of letters who were his friends. This was a famous meeting of literary heroes and the two poets immediately took to one another, thereafter meeting almost daily, while Scott remained in London, at John Murray's offices: John Murray the second, then a boy, remembered them stumping downstairs side by side.

When the two met, the venerable Scott was forty-three; Byron was twenty-seven, though this fascinating rebel was already "the idol of the sentimental part of society" and quite widely travelled. They must have been entertaining meetings: both had humour and loved fun; both knew much of the world.

In addition to the meetings at John Murray's, they also frequently attended the same parties in the evenings. Captain Gronow describes a dinner-time meeting between Scott and Byron in the autumn of 1815: he tells us that Scott was "quite delightful, full of fire and animation"; Byron was "in great good humour, and full of boyish and even boisterous mirth".

The last meeting on September 14th, 1815 must have been characterised by similar joviality. It is clear from the letter that Scott wrote to Byron's biographer Tom Moore that it was Byron's light-heartedness which impressed him. "I saw Byron for the last time in 1815," he wrote. "He dined or lunched with me at Long's, in Bond Street. I never saw him so full of gaiety and good humour, to which the presence of Mr Mathews, the comedian, added not a little. Poor Terry was also present." Their number, in addition to Charles Mathews and Daniel Terry, included Scott's young kinsman, John Scott of Gala, who had recorded in his notebook this most interesting day he ever spent. But to him Byron appeared sardonic. "How I did stare," he says, "at Byron's beautiful pale face, like a spirit's – good or evil. But he was *bitter* – what a contrast to Scott! Among other anecdotes of British prowess and spirit, Scott mentioned that a young gentleman – – – had been awfully shot in the head while conveying an order from the Duke, and yet staggered on, and delivered his message when at the point of death. 'Ha!' said Byron, 'I daresay he could do as well as most people without his head – it was never of much use to him.' Waterloo did not delight him, probably – and Scott could talk or think of scarcely anything else."

Before they parted for the last time Scott and Byron exchanged gifts

Sir Walter Scott and Lord Byron met for the last time at Long's Hotel

Long's Hotel in New Bond Street, one of the men-only "sporting" hotels of Mayfair

"like the old heroes in Homer," as Scott put it. He gave Byron a Turkish dagger; Byron gave him a silver vase full of dead men's bones. They laughed at what the world would think of their sombre gifts, exchanged in so pleasant a mood.

Byron also had other associations with Bond Street, one connection being his membership of the Pugilistic Club, kept by Gentleman Jackson, who was champion bare-fist boxer of England until defeated by Mendoza. The two then together formed the Bond Street Club. Byron was a great frequenter of Bond Street, often attending parties at the Pugilistic Club, Long's Hotel or Steven's Hotel, and he also stayed at those two hotels at various times. Tom Moore tells us that Steven's, which was just two doors from Long's, at 18 New Bond Street, was one of Byron's "old haunts" in the days when he was determinedly living a fashionable life, consorting with the finest dandies of the town.

At this time Steven's Hotel (which was later to become Fischer's) was fashionable as the headquarters for army officers and men about town. Captain Gronow tells us in his *Reminiscences* that if a stranger wanted to dine there, he would be "stared at by the servants and very solemnly assured that there was no table vacant". He adds that it was not uncommon to see thirty or even forty saddle-horses or tilburies waiting outside the doors of this hotel, and that two of his old Welsh friends who stayed here in 1815 qualified themselves for residence by "disposing of five bottles of wine daily" – whether together or each is not stated.

Another great poet associated with Bond Street was Percy Bysshe Shelley (1792–1822), who stayed at 15 Old Bond Street, just opposite Stafford Street, in 1814, when things were going badly between him and his wife, his father and his finances.

Having been sent down from Oxford for circulating a pamphlet on "The Necessity of Atheism", that same year he married Harriet Westbrook, then only sixteen, from whom he was to separate after three years of itinerant wanderings. He was much under the influence of

Percy Bysshe Shelley, another of Bond Street's great literary men, who spent an unsettled few months here in 1814

Saddle horses in Bond Street – a sight once familiar in days of less hectic traffic

William Godwin and his long poem *Queen Mab*, written at this time, has been described as "Godwin versified". Of Harriet's unhappy life during these years we know little. It was possibly her insistence on a remarriage in church in 1814 which led to the final breach in the spring of that year and, two years later, to her tragic death in the Serpentine.

Poor Harriet, intelligent and well-read, and deeply in love with Shelley, did her best to understand his enthusiasms and ideals; but she could not share them. She paid a long visit to Bath while he lodged in Bond Street and spent most of his time at the house of the revolutionary Godwin, free to cultivate the friendship of his daughter Mary Wollstonecraft. Free love was part of the Godwinian ideology and in July 1814 Shelley left for Europe with her (they were later to marry after Harriet's death), returning six weeks later. Soon after this, in September 1814, Shelley's grandfather died and the poet became heir to a large estate, successfully bargaining with his father for an income of £1,000 a year.

Shelley was one of those rare people who lived his life entirely by his own rules, oblivious to any condemnation: personal attacks neither embittered nor changed him. Passionate, volatile and, though certainly not heartless, completely heedless of others, he nevertheless had a sublime beauty of character and expression which, for later generations if not his own, has lifted him above criticism.

Bond Street, as time progressed through the settled and satisfied days of Queen Victoria, remained all it had ever been to the world of fashion, at the same time becoming a great unseen upholder of the *status quo*. Its shops were offering an increasing abundance of rich treasures born of a new mechanised age though, compared to the commercial excesses of the late twentieth century, these shops still had a leisurely and personal intimacy which looked back rather than forward. Courtly shopkeepers who still lived above their shops could offer their rich clients endless hours of service by day and courteous entertainment in their dining-rooms at night.

In 1879 the attractions of Bond Street were expanded into the Arcade, lined with about twenty shops and linking Old Bond Street and Albemarle Street. After Queen Victoria herself had patronised the hosier and shirt-maker, H. W. Bretell, from whom she bought riding shirts, knitting wool and large plain linen handkerchiefs, and the florists Goodyear's, it became the Royal Arcade, surviving today despite a bad bombing in 1940.

Queen Victoria, who for many years had been little seen in the streets of London, began, towards the end of her life, to make more frequent appearances in the thoroughfares of the West End. One afternoon in the 'nineties she put in a stately appearance in Bond Street for the first time in twenty-five years, which set the whole street agog. The wealthy traders and their customers, hearing and then seeing the outriders and equerries clattering along the road, heralding the grand entrance of the Sovereign herself, could scarcely believe their eyes.

Mrs E. T. Cook, in her *Highways and Byways of London*, published in 1902, recalled late Victorian Bond Street as a place where the poor could rub shoulders with the rich. At that time there was still an "expensive fish-shop in Bond Street – where, during long summer days, enormous blocks of ice, tempting to the eye, glitter like some Rajah's diamond" and which "entertains a motley crew of poor folk on Saturday nights, when it makes a practice of giving away its remaining stock."

"Here, at four o'clock or so in the afternoon," were still "to be seen the 'gilded youth' – the dandies of the day – here the smart world flock for afternoon tea; and here fine ladies walk even unattended, and satisfy . . . their feminine cravings for shop-windows. Who was it who first said that no real woman could ever pass a hat-shop? The truth of this remark may be here attested. The very smartest of motor-cars – of horses – of 'turn-outs' generally – may be seen blocking the narrow Piccadilly entrance of this thoroughfare . . ."

Two views of Bond Street at the turn of the century

It was now, as much as ever before, the "street of London's charms the centre", about whose fine shops Lord Beaconsfield once waxed eloquent, and in which was segregated the very best of brilliant humanity.

Edward Walford, in *Old and New London* (1897) describes the shops of New Bond Street at the close of the nineteenth century as "extremely elegant", while "the articles exhibited for sale are of the most *recherché* description". He selects the most notable for special reference. "At the corner of Bruton Street", he tells us, "is the shop of Mr C. Hannocks, the great manufacturing jeweller. At 156 are the showrooms of Messrs Hunt & Roskell . . . At No. 160 were the extensive show-rooms of Messrs Copeland & Co. (formerly Messrs Copeland & Spode), the eminent porcelain manufacturers, of Stoke-on-Trent, almost the only rivals of Messrs Wedgwood . . . "

The invention of the sewing-machine in the middle of the nineteenth century inaugurated what was to be the immensely important ready-made clothing business and by 1866 Redmayne & Company of 19 and 20 New Bond Street were advertising made-up skirts for walking.

Later in the century, needlework of a more old-fashioned type was offered by a surprising individual. The beautiful, privileged philan-thropist, Lady Brooke, the Countess of Warwick, an embracer of Socialism and untiring champion of the underdog, had an interesting connection with Bond Street. She was much concerned, at the begin-ning of the 1890s, with the disastrous agricultural depression in Essex, and in particular with the unhappy plight of those young village girls in their early teens who left school and, because of delicate health or physical handicaps, could not undertake the heavy tasks demanded from general household servants – then almost the only opportunity of employment. To provide jobs using the one skill they usually did leave school with, that for intricate needlework, Lady Brooke opened a needlework school at Easton Lodge, her mansion in Essex, where the high wages she paid soon attracted more than enough little would-

89

The Countess of Warwick's needlework shop in Bond Street *c.* 1900

At a meeting of the London Sketch Club in Bond Street *c.* 1901 are three famous members, Cecil Aldin, Phil May and Dudley Hardy

be needlewomen, frail and robust alike. The output of fine articles soon exceeding the demand from her immediate circle of friends, the Countess of Warwick took the revolutionary step, in 1891, of opening a shop in Bond Street: "Lady Brooke's depot for the Easton school of Needlework", its sign read. Malicious gossip bubbled up through polite society already critical of her private life: trade was despised and many a nose was looked down at her "taking up shop" – especially as she was actually observed serving behind the counter herself. The Bond Street "shop" was in fact, in the beginning, only a show-room for samples of articles made at the school, where orders and measurements were taken. The hubbub of social condemnation at least had the advantage of publicising the brave scheme: soon the Bond Street depot, employing "ladies in reduced circumstances" as well as fully trained girls from Easton, was extended to include a workroom where elaborate tea-gowns were made on the premises. The depot remained open for a decade, closing in 1901: it had been a brave attempt at solving the bottomless problem of poverty in a small but sympathetic and useful way.

Bond Street's connection with the world of art was extremely important in Victorian days. Edward Walford mentions some of the interesting establishments of New Bond Street, both small and large. "At No. 116 in this street," he tells us, "Miss Clark, the great-granddaughter of Theodore, King of Corsica . . . was established as a miniature-painter early in the present century . . .

"Dealers in pictures and other branches of the fine arts are numerous in this street; besides which the picture galleries offer opportunities for a pleasing promenade for such as care to avail themselves of them. Foremost among these was the Doré Gallery, situated at No. 35. The Doré collection, which included some of the choicest productions of the distinguished French artist, M. Gustave Doré, was for many years open daily all the year round . . .

"At No. 47 is the Hanover Gallery, frequently used for the exhibition of pictures. No. 136 [later 135] was the Grosvenor Gallery, which from 1875 to 1890 was one of the popular exhibitions of the 'season', the pictures shown here being principally of the 'aesthetic' school. Scores of exhibitions of pictures and other curiosities, too numerous to particularise, have at various times existed in New Bond Street and its neighbourhood."

Bond Street is, of course, still noted for its picture galleries, though the once famous Grosvenor Gallery has gone. W. W. Hutchings, in *London Town Past and Present* (1909) sketches its history: "The Grosvenor Gallery is now put to other uses than those it was built to subserve . . . The creation of Sir Coutts Lindsay, artist and man of fortune [its fine entrance was by Palladio of Venice and its front was designed by Soames], it was opened in 1877 as a picture gallery where, to quote from Lady Burne-Jones's *Memorials* of her husband, 'distrust of originality and imagination would not be shown, delicate workmanship would not be extinguished, and the number of pictures exhibited would not be too large for the wall-space.' The building is believed to have cost upwards of £100,000, and the first show was made memorable by the inclusion of several of the works of Burne-Jones, who had never before exhibited at a public gallery. In his opinion it was far from being an ideal picture gallery, for he thought its sumptuous hangings, its gilding and ornamental features generally were superfluous and out of place, but to several successive exhibitions he sent his pictures, until in 1887 he wrote to his friend Mr Charles Hallé, protesting against innovations of the preceding season. 'Club rooms, concert rooms, and the rest,' he urged, 'were not in the plan,' and must and would degrade the Gallery. 'One night we are a background for tobacco and another for flirting – excellent things both, but then not there.' The letter was endorsed by Mr Hallé and Mr Comyns Carr, who both retired from the direction of the Gallery, and Burne-Jones also severed his connection with it."

Another New Bond Street gallery was the Modern Gallery at No.

175, where the London Sketch Club (now at Dilke Street in Chelsea) held its inaugural Exhibition, and its first working meetings. "A Lay-Member" amusingly reported in *The Art Record* of May 11th, 1901: "There are other things besides art at the London Sketch Club, though they really shouldn't be spoken of, for, on the authority of a no less person than the president, Mr George Haité, the London Sketch Club is founded, more or less, for the express purpose of correcting several wrong notions about art that have been growing wild in the public mind. Therefore, if from the point of view of a mere literary associate, the members don't always toe the line in the earnest endeavour to prove that art is really the only thing worth living for, it isn't the president's fault.

"The fact is, there is a lot of youthful exuberance on the club's books, and so when it begins to effervesce, the bubbles are large and coloury.

"Every Friday night the members meet at the Modern Gallery, Bond Street, and are good for exactly two hours, while they slap colour on as hard as they can."

After "the whistle is blown at nine o'clock" the "other things besides art" are indulged in. "On one memorable evening, Tom Browne was induced to sing. His voice had long lain dormant and fallow, but it being an occasion when everyone was doing his utmost to help along the harmony of the evening, he rose to do his best. Scarce had he got to the third line of the first verse, when, by a most cruel, preconceived plan, the assembled members rose hurriedly and stampeded through the door."

Members were keen caricaturists and cartoonists. "It is not always wise to enter the barbarous precincts of the club in evening-dress," warns Lay-Member. "Several individuals did so upon a certain occasion. But very little time had elapsed when their immaculate shirt-fronts were covered with drawings like the pages of a sketch-book. Almost immediately, the wheeze, which had been intended to

93

annoy rather than please, leapt into sudden popularity, so that those who were unadorned, immediately sought such decoration, and pretty quickly every shirt-front was drawn or scrawled over. One individual declared that he intended to cut out the front from the shirt for the purpose of framing it, and, considering it bore signed drawings by Phil May, Dudley Hardy, Tom Browne, Hassall, Sauber, Cecil Aldin, and others as famous, the notion was reasonable."

Phil May, the black and white artist, in fact lived at one time in Bond Street. Lay-Member has another anecdote about him too: "Phil May once made a famous speech. He arose with great ceremony, and gravely taking out a pair of spectacles, adjusted them on his nose with much gravity. He then coughed, and paused while he placed a pair of pince-nez over his spectacles. Having done this, he coughed again, and looked around, then taking out another pair of glasses, put them on also. The members now sat waiting anxiously. He beamed through his various spectacles upon them, and then opened his mouth, but didn't speak, because he suddenly felt in a pocket and found there some more spectacles, which he similarly placed over the others. This went on for some time, always opening his mouth to speak, and then pausing to put on another pair of spectacles, until he had no less than seven or eight pairs. Then he spoke at last. He said: 'Tut-tut!' and sat down gravely."

The list of inhabitants of Bond Street in 1886 reveals an interesting name at 160 New Bond Street: that of the explorer and journalist, Henry Morton Stanley (1841–1904). He won fame in 1871 after the *New York Herald* had sent him to Tanganyika with the laconic brief: "Find Livingstone." During 1879 he established the Congo Free State under the auspices of the Belgian King, and was to embark on his final expedition to central Africa after his sojourn in Bond Street. His large, expensively furnished flat in New Bond Street was used as a store for the tents, scientific apparatus and other equipment he was avidly collecting for the coming expedition.

The most illustrious of Bond Street's inhabitants at this time,

The great Henry Irving, Bond Street's last famous inhabitant, in his role as Mathias

"Making a few necessary but attractive purchases in Bond Street" – an elegant shopper of 1904 steps from her carriage

however, was the great actor Sir Henry Irving (1838–1905), who had rooms at the corner of Bond Street and Grafton Street between 1872 and 1899, above Asprey's. Though Shaw dismissed him as having "simply no brains, all character and temperament", he did not in fact attempt to project the poignancy of passion of the genuine emotional actor. Beneath the exaggerated mannerisms and rather thin and hard voice, however, his interpretation of subtle emotions and motives was brilliant. His famous theatrical partnership with Ellen Terry began in 1878 and continued till 1902, and he was, during these years, actor-manager-lessee of the Lyceum.

By the autumn of 1877 Irving's fame was such that he earned a profile in the "Celebrities at Home" feature in the *World*, which includes an amusing and most interesting description of his rooms, where "He has pitched his tent within the busy haunts of men, and elaborates his studies of the creations of the Bard of Avon, within cry of St James's Street clubs." Irving's extraordinary study, "his sanctum, the room in which he sits deep into the night, reading or musing or chatting", is described in the following terms: "It has a somewhat sombre air; for the London sunlight, never too brilliant, is further modified by having to find its way through windows of stained glass, and there are evidences that the sacrilegious brush of the housemaid is never permitted within the precincts. Nowhere could be found a more perfect example of the confusion and neglect of order in which the artistic mind delights. It is visible everywhere – in the yawning gaps in the bookshelves, from which the volumes now strewing the floor have been hastily dragged for reference or study; in the rucks and folds of the huge tiger-skin rug, which has suffered grievously under the impatient trampings of its owner; in the table pushed on one side, and groaning under its accumulated litter of books, prints, manuscripts – what an enormous amount of dormant talent may there not be in these manuscripts with which a favourite actor is so constantly pelted! – its blotting-book, gaping inkstand, and *chevaux de frise* of pens. The piano

Sketch design by Frank Brangwyn, A.R.A., for the decoration of Bond
Street on the occasion of the coronation of King George V, June 22nd,
1911

97

The blitz on Bond Street – an aftermath of rubble left by a night of
bombing during the Second World War

is opened . . . At the foot of the music-stool is a large brown paper package, obviously containing boxes of cigars, and bearing the name of a well-known tobacconist in Pall Mall; a Louis Quinze clock ticks from an unsuspected corner; a few antique chairs shrug their high shoulders, as though completely overwhelmed by the confusion; and the broad sofa seems, from the variety of its contents, to have lost its identity, and to be undecided whether it was intended for a wardrobe, a bookcase, or a portfolio."

Irving himself is equally cleverly portrayed: "The owner of these rooms is just now one of the best-known men in London. As he jerks along the street with league-devouring stride, his long, dark hair hanging over his shoulders, his look dreamy and absent, his cheeks wan and thin, the slovenly air with which his clothes are worn in contrast with their fashionable cut, people turn to stare after him and tell each other who he is."

And so to modern Bond Street, for many years now famous for its luxury clothes, its jewellers, its picture galleries and other worthy establishments. Despite the clamour of twentieth-century hurry and traffic it is still exclusive and still elegant, a bright spot in a world of deteriorating standards, a last bastion against the shabby greyness of unscrupulous mass production, its precious heritage of prestige and worth guarded by its Bond Street Association.

The fascinating catalogue of famous inhabitants has now, sadly, dried up as the exigencies of commerce have driven out the private lodger. The shops are now supreme, business eclipsing even entertainment, though in the 1930s, the time of the great Mayfair night-clubs, the Embassy in Old Bond Street brought fame by being a favourite haunt of the late Duke of Windsor when he was Prince of Wales.

Though some of Bond Street's old buildings have survived, the re-buildings of latter days have been extensive. Tallis's *London Street Views* of about 1840, which include elevations of Old and New Bond Streets, present a relatively harmonious aspect with terraces of square Georgian

99

buildings. By 1880 the character of Bond Street was changing, however. *The Building News* that year reported: "In Bond Street a few disciples of the fashionable school have already made a mark, for here and there, among the ordinary and commonplace fronts, are seen a few in red brick in Queen Anne, or a style that looks very like it. . . . Altogether, New Bond Street presents a curious mixture of Italian Renaissance, Jacobean, and Gothic features. . . . We look in vain, however, for any new building of quiet dignity or merit. Those recently built suggest the idea of cramming into mere strips of frontages all the detail that can be forced on to them, and we cannot avoid the reflection that, in another age, many of them will be viewed in the light of burlesques." These new Victorian buildings had disrupted the homogeneity of the Georgian street, and later architecture became increasingly diverse so that today there is an inharmonious conglomeration of old and new. However, most of it is low-key and it is not an unpleasing mixture – Bond Street has, in any case, never been remarkable for its buildings, being, in David Piper's phrase, "as it were above architecture". There is no ostentatious grandeur here, only a solid accumulation of dignity and worth presented in a rather off-hand manner which is thoroughly English.

Modern Bond Street is not over modern: it is resistant to change, wisely cherishing its heritage. The suggestion that the "Old" and "New" of the name be dropped was scornfully rejected by local ratepayers in the late 'forties, and the crazy numbering where the two sections meet continues.

Bond Street's traffic problems, which already caused concern in the early nineteenth century, have not been ameilorated by modern habits. Harold P. Clunn in *The Face of London* (Spring Books) describes the trials of the early 'fifties, which were to grow a lot worse: "Opposite Grafton Street, Old Bond Street narrows into a tiresome bottleneck, which might aptly be christened the Straits of Bond Street, and which exercises a stranglehold on the heavy traffic of this thoroughfare.

Sometimes a long line of omnibuses and motor-cars is held up by stationary vehicles in this immediate locality. Whilst many people will be aghast at the very suggestion that this small section of Bond Street should be widened at enormous expense, yet taking a long view of the pressing requirements of London's traffic, even this improvement might not be incommensurate with the cost which would be incurred. So great is the traffic congestion caused by stationary motor-cars during the day-time in this part of the West End that its streets seem like one gigantic garage. The blitzed sites of New Bond Street have been put to temporary use as car parks."

The blitzed sites are now built on, but no hand was sacrilegious enough to widen the Straits of Bond Street: instead the thoroughfare has been blocked off by trees in tubs, and the traffic continues to gush along, though Bond Street can at least no longer complain of being one of the West End's major waste channels for through traffic.

Today the fine establishments of Bond Street which have won world-wide renown are very many indeed. In the following pages we shall look at the history of the best known of them, businesses whose endeavours have continued a proud tradition in this most worthy of the great streets of London.

Chapter Four

FAMOUS NAMES IN BOND STREET

*   *   *

As we have seen in earlier chapters, Bond Street has for long been famous for its shops. Once they were small, if select, businesses, serving little more than their immediate neighbourhood, and supplying a far wider cross-section of daily requirements than did the more sophisticated establishments of later years.

Even by about 1840, when Tallis's list of the occupants of the street was compiled, it is interesting to note that most of Bond Street's traders were already dealing in fashion and luxury merchandise. Apart from purveyors of various types of foodstuffs, major categories the shop-keepers of this period fell into were tailors (there were twenty-two of these – as many as food shops of all kinds put together), hatters, boot and shoemakers, perfumers, dealers in lace and silks, and wine and spirit merchants.

Later the humble fish shops and bakeries disappeared, to be replaced by more grandiose emporiums serving not just Mayfair but the whole of fashionable London. By Victorian times many of the famous houses of Bond Street which are household words today had already been established. Lord Beaconsfield in *Lothair* (1871) paints a fine picture of the delights that could then be expected from Bond Street's shops: "there is no street in the world that can furnish such a collection, filled with so many objects of beauty, curiosity, and interest. The jewellers and goldsmiths and dealers in rare furniture, porcelain, and cabinets, and French pictures, have long fixed upon Bond Street as their favourite quarter, and are not chary of displaying their treasures; though it may be a question whether some of the magazines of fancy food, delicacies rolled from all the climes and regions of the globe, particularly at the matin hour, may not, in their picturesque vanity, be the most attractive."

Of Bond Street traders of the more traditional variety there are still a large number today. Though purveyors of foodstuffs are now few, the world of fashion, especially ladies' fashion, is still exceedingly well represented, with a large number of firms specialising in knitwear and footwear. Hats, however, are *passé*: the supremacy of Bond Street's hatters and milliners has been brought low by modern trends. Of cosmetics and beauty experts, however, there are still many. And the goldsmiths, silversmiths, jewellers, dealers in fine leather goods and furriers still abound, while there are over twenty fine art dealers.

These are all established types in Bond Street, but there are newcomers, too, offering a sophisticated range of modern services mostly undreamt of in earlier times. Occupying the upper floors of many of Bond Street's desirable addresses are now a profusion of "Consultants" – property consultants, investment consultants, finance, business and marketing consultants, training consultants, sales promotion consultants, public relations consultants. . . . The profferers of select services are supreme: there are lawyers, engineers, surveyors, accountants, estate agents, insurance brokers and half a dozen banks. There are something like thirty-five employment agencies and personnel consultants. Tourism is now big business in Bond Street: there are some twenty tour operators, travel agents and tourist offices, and over a dozen airline offices. In another topical field, there are now ten companies in Bond Street connected with the North Sea oil industry.

All the benefits of modern commerce have served to expand the influence of Bond Street's establishments; many today serve not just London but the world. Yet there tend to linger old-fashioned ethics and

Sotheby's famous entrance at 34 & 35 New Bond Street in *c.* 1920, soon after their establishment here

standards of excellence, old-fashioned courtesy, and many proud family traditions.

In looking at some of the most renowned firms in Bond Street today, we begin with one whose fame is indeed worldwide: at 34 and 35 New Bond Street is Sotheby's, the oldest and the largest fine art auction house in the world. Founded in 1744 by the London bookseller Samuel Baker, it specialised first in the sale of rare books: by 1800 the firm had become the leading book auctioneers of the world, while during the following century regular sales of prints, pictures, antiquities, jewellery, coins, wine and furniture were also held.

In 1917 the firm moved from Wellington Street, where it had been established for a century, to its New Bond Street headquarters, premises which had formerly housed the Doré Gallery, where the pictures of the great illustrator Gustave Doré had formerly been exhibited. In these famous rooms, with their modest entrance, described by Pevsner as "demonstratively undemonstrative", Sotheby's have prospered, and in growing have been fundamental in establishing London as the centre of the world art market.

It was in 1954, with the removal of restrictions on the import of fine art objects from the United States and the re-establishment of Sotheby's right to pay the proceeds of sales in the consignor's own currency, that the company's rapid international expansion began, an office being opened in New York the following year. In 1958, in one of the most famous auctions of modern times, which changed the face of the international art world, seven Impressionist paintings from the collection of Jakob Goldschmidt of New York were sold for £781,000, Cezanne's "Garcon au Gilet Rouge" fetching a record £220,000 – small beer in modern terms, but then more than double the previous record. At the news of this sale the world art market leapt overnight to life: fine art auctions entered the first league of big business and newsworthiness, while London had become their unquestioned capital.

Since then Sotheby's business interests abroad have expanded rapidly; in 1964 the Parke Bernet Galleries of New York, America's biggest fine art auctioneers, were acquired. Today Sotheby's operates in twenty-one countries and has auction rooms in ten of them; a thousand sales are held a year all over the world. The annual turnover is in the region of £163 million, and ever rising. In May 1977 the sale of the contents of Mentmore Towers realised £6,389,933, *ten* times the previous record for any house sale, while more recently records have been broken by the sale of the von Hirsch collection, which made £18,468,348.

The auctioneers Phillips have occupied their premises at Blenstock House, in Blenheim Street, off New Bond Street, since 1939; before that they had been established at 73 (earlier 68) New Bond Street from 1797, the year after they were founded, and until that building (one of Bond Street's last original Georgian houses) was destroyed by fire in July 1939. Harry Phillips was their founder, a shrewd businessman and also a happy dabbler in London society, who staged fashionable *soirées* as preludes to important sales. Many were the notable men of his day who bought and sold through him, as Basil Boothroyd points out in his lively booklet *Twenty Thousand Sales by Phillips*: "When he sold the Bruton Street possessions of George 'Beau' Brummell, for instance, two marquesses, five lords and their ladies (including Grey, the Prime Minister) were among the buyers. He sold for the Duke of Buckingham . . . the Duke of Roxburgh, the Earl of Kent, deceased (the catalogue of his wines tastefully bordered in black), for George IV, for Lady Hertford, Prince Talleyrand, Prince Lieven, Lord Charles Somerset. . . ." The fascinating catalogue of customers and merchandise was to continue into modern times, enlivened by unthought-of-hitherto prices and the unpredictable fads of modern collectors.

Other auctioneers of a more specialised sort are Harmers of London at 41 New Bond Street, whose name is synonymous with the most lucrative transactions in the rarefied world of philately. Their founder, H. R. Harmer, a childhood convert to this fascinating preoccupation,

The catalogue of one of Phillips' prestigious early sales

The old Phillips' premises at 73 New Bond Street, the last of the Bond Street residential fronts

held his first stamp auction in 1918 at 6, 7 and 8 Old Bond Street, which brought in a modest £1,228. Since then over four thousand sessions of auctions have been held, each sale averaging over £100,000 and contributing to an annual turnover of two-and-a-half million, while Harmers International, still a family concern, has today spread its wings to expanding markets in the United States and Australia.

As already mentioned, fine art dealers are now, and have long been, of major importance in Bond Street. A glance at the lists of inhabitants at different times reveals many famous names in the art world, some remaining, some gone. It is interesting to note "Duveen Brothers, Experts in Works of Art" at 21 Old Bond Street in 1911. It was at the end of the 1880s that Joel Duveen (father of the legendary Joseph, later Lord Duveen of Millbank) and his brother Henry opened a new gallery in Old Bond Street, already the world's centre of trade in old masters. With the employment of one of the two Dowdeswell brothers, who had just left his own firm of high-class picture dealers in New Bond Street, the Duveen Brothers' Gallery soon became one of the world's most important. In 1938 we may see "John Duveen, Art Expert" at 160 New Bond Street. And there are a great number of illustrious names which survive today, of which just a few may be mentioned here.

The firm of P. & D. Colnaghi & Co. Ltd, "Experts, valuers and dealers in paintings, drawings, engravings and etchings", are today established at 14 Old Bond Street. In the latter part of the eighteenth century, an energetic young Italian from Milan with a flair for art dealing, Paul Colnaghi, was employed in Paris by Anthony Torre to manage one branch of the business his father had established, which at that time also dealt in books and scientific instruments. In 1785 Colnaghi moved to the London base of the firm which three years later he took over upon Torre's retirement.

Despite the trials of the Napoleonic Wars, Colnaghi's business flourished, winning the patronage of the English court and members of the exiled French court. His eldest son Dominic proved an able assistant and successor: by the middle of the nineteenth century the firm had become one of the foremost publishers of prints, an activity which, however, had less importance by the end of the century due to the advent of new photographic methods of picture reproduction. However, the publication of etchings and dry-points continued and these were popular until the 1930s. In addition to these ventures, the Old Master side of the business was greatly expanded.

In 1912 the firm moved to large new premises specially built for them at 144–6 New Bond Street. Of many fine art collections acquired by Colnaghi's, probably the most spectacular of all was that from the Hermitage Museum, purchased from the Soviet government in 1930–1. Included were works by van Eyck, Botticelli, Raphael, Rubens, Rembrandt and Tiepolo, many of which found their way to Washington, D.C. Today Colnaghi's vast stock is made readily accessible to the art-loving public by regular, well-documented exhibitions on particular themes held in their new premises at 14 Old Bond Street.

The galleries originally built for Colnaghi in the early part of this century at 144–6 New Bond Street, have, since 1943, been occupied by Partridge (Fine Arts) Limited, who moved in at a time when they were being used as a Night Wardens' Shelter. The firm's founder, Frank Partridge – whose grandson is the present Chairman – was Personal Adviser to Her Majesty Queen Mary, and was awarded her Royal Warrant.

At 148 New Bond Street is the Fine Art Society which, since it was established at these very premises (once a grocer's shop over which the crazed Lord Camelford had lodgings) in 1876, has been one of the leading picture galleries in Bond Street. Founded with the purpose of exhibiting and publishing copies of pictures by British artists, and later also books on art, the reputation of the Society was soon established through the quality of its well-documented exhibitions, including those of Millais and Holman Hunt in 1881 and 1886 respectively which won a tremendous public response. In its early years Ruskin, Whistler, E. W. Godwin and Millais were all closely associated with the Fine Art Society, which was eagerly promoting public interest in art and also giving minor artists the opportunity to exhibit.

In 1881 the architect E. W. Godwin was commissioned to alter the plain Georgian front of the Fine Art Society's premises "and make it rather less of a shop front": his bold and highly original design was hailed by *The Art Journal* as "the most telling and commanding entrance in the whole of Bond Street" – indeed its impact must have been considerable on a street then still largely made up of plain Georgian facades. Godwin's new front is still a great source of pride to the Fine Art Society, who see in it "a physical expression of the aims of the Society; the vestibule with its exhibition cabinets encourages one to linger and enter the galleries; the overhead balcony . . . enhances this feeling of intimacy and curiosity."

Wildenstein & Company, the fine art dealers at 147 New Bond Street, have a plaque pointing out that it was at this site that Nelson lodged in 1797, in the house, then numbered 141, where James Thomson had earlier lived. Though Wildenstein have been in Bond Street only since 1936, the company was founded back in 1875, in Paris, since which time galleries have also been opened in New York, Buenos Aires and Tokyo. The varied activities of the firm over the years have included the organisation of many international exhibitions and the purchasing of large private collections: among its clients are the world's foremost collectors and museums.

Agnew's Galleries, well stocked with a wide variety of paintings, drawings and engravings, are at 43 Old Bond Street, and owe their origin to Thomas Agnew who, early in the nineteenth century, joined the art business of Vittore Zanetti in Manchester, soon becoming a partner – to be succeeded by nine other Agnews. The present Galleries, built on the site of an old coaching yard, were opened in 1876; since the closure of the Manchester office in 1932 they have been the head-

E. W. Godwin's impressive front
to the Fine Art Society's building
at 148 New Bond Street

The entrance gallery of the Fine
Art Society as redecorated in
1888 by George Faulkner
Armitage

quarters of the business. W. W. Hutchings in his *London Town Past and Present* (1909) records that these galleries were "the scene, in 1876, of the theft of Gainsborough's Duchess of Devonshire. The picture was the talk of the town from the price – 10,100 guineas – it fetched at Christie's, the highest price ever paid at an auction for a portrait; and one morning, when the gallery in which it was being exhibited was opened, the frame was found empty. The theory of the police was that the theft was the work of some visitor to the exhibition who had contrived to secrete himself on the premises at closing time, and slipped out when the doors were opened next morning. No one was brought to book for the theft, although Messrs Agnew offered a reward of a thousand pounds; but after remaining *perdu* for years the stolen treasure mysteriously turned up in 1901 and was recovered by or restored to its owners."

Today the firm of Thomas Agnew & Sons is in the hands of four managing directors, all descended either directly or by marriage from Thomas Angew. The famous Galleries have, over the years, played host to many great exhibitions. Today there are annual showings of Old Master paintings and eighteenth- and ninteenth-century water-colours, as well as works of twentieth-century English painters, while Loan Exhibitions in aid of charity are also regular events.

At 41 New Bond Street are the fine Galleries of Messrs Frost & Reed. Back in the reign of George III, Mr Reed established his business in Bristol, amalgamating with that of Mr Frost towards the end of the nineteenth century. Though its West Country links have always been maintained, Bond Street is now the headquarters of the company. Over the years many of Britain and the world's foremost works of art have passed through its Galleries – also the scene of important exhibitions. Among the many fine prints they have issued are reproductions of water-colours by Sir William Russell Flint, the celebrated Royal Academician, who died in 1969 in his ninetieth year. The activities of Frost & Reed include what is now a flourishing export business, grown to a million-dollar industry since those now far-off days when Walter Frost first crossed the Atlantic in 1894.

At 40 New Bond Street are Mallett & Son, "Dealers in the finest English and Continental antique furniture," founded in Bath in 1865 by the jeweller and silversmith John Mallett, whose son Walter expanded his stock into the realms of old silver and furniture, now the company's foremost interest. After a successful participation in the Franco-British Exhibition at Earls Court in 1908 it was decided to open a shop in London, and the premises in New Bond Street was leased; in 1937, after the death of Walter Mallett, the whole business moved to London where, behind a "discreet facade" lie "eleven spacious rooms filled with eighteenth-century furniture".

The world-famous china and glass store at 19 South Audley Street, Thomas Goode & Company, celebrated its 150th anniversary in 1977, this esteemed family business having been established by Thomas Goode "chinaman" in 1827. Since that time it is justly proud of having "contributed much to the development of good taste in ceramics of all kinds" – and indeed the beautiful pieces bearings its own famous stamp are highly valued by collectors. Although the main showrooms are still in South Audley Street, additional premises were acquired at 2 Old Bond Street in 1972: between them the two establishments today house what is considered to be the finest collection in the world of quality bone china, crystal and continental glass, and contemporary table ware, as well as other gift items, chandeliers and table lamps.

At 50 New Bond Street is the Chappell Music Centre, offering "departments devoted to each aspect of music". It was Samuel Chappell who, early in the nineteenth century, established himself as a music publisher, seller of fine pianos and promoter of musical performances, and who soon gained a sturdy reputation. The business was moved to 124 New Bond Street in 1811, where, in 1819, it was commended by no less a master than Beethoven himself, who, writing from Vienna to his friend Ferdinand Ries in London about the prospect of publishing a piano sonata and a string quartette, says he has heard that "Chappell of Bond Street is now one of the best publishers."

In 1830 Chappell's moved to the present site at 50 New Bond Street, where their old-time building figured in *Tallis's Street Views* (1840–1). After the death of Samuel Chappell in 1834, the business was carried on by his widow, Emily, and sons, William and Thomas. In addition to efforts on behalf of the art of music, it was also Tom Chappell who organised those immensely successful readings by Charles Dickens of his popularly acclaimed novels. The first series of tours was a triumph, though the success of the second was unfortunately interrupted by the novelist's ill health. Dickens expressed great appreciation of the manner in which the tours had been organised by Chappells, and, when plans for the second series were upset, their "noble and munificent manner of sweeping away into space all the charges incurred uselessly" much impressed him.

Over the years a great number of famous works have been published by Chappells, including Gilbert and Sullivan's immortal "Savoy Operas". Today the publishing tradition is proudly continued, while Chappell & Company are now also renowned as the manufacturers of quality pianos.

In the Tallis lists of about 1840, five goldsmiths or silversmiths are mentioned. Today there are over twenty, including the exclusive establishment of S. J. Phillips, "where exquisitely worked and timeless jewellery from the Czar's Court can be found, as well as priceless tiaras, rings, and brooches from many other lands." At 111–12 New Bond Street are the Bond Street Silver Galleries, where numerous firms exhibit on three floors valuable silverwork of astonishing beauty.

Asprey's with its exceptionally fine mid-Victorian shop-front and plaque to remind us that the great Henry Irving once paced its upper floor, is at 165–9 New Bond Street, premises which probably date back to the end of the previous century. This firm was founded in Mitcham in 1781 by William Asprey, the descendant of a distinguished Huguenot family, who, a century earlier, had brought their many skills – they were silversmiths, watchmakers, weavers, calico printers, leather workers and master smiths – to England when they fled from France. William Asprey, himself a fine metal worker, and his son, Charles, built up a flourishing business, the best success of which was the manufacture of fitted dressing cases, soon to become an indispensable luxury of the fashionable.

In the 1830s Charles Asprey moved his already prestigious firm to more appropriate premises at 49 New Bond Street, setting up there as a dressing-case maker and fine stationer. By 1848 he was ready to move to larger premises at 166 New Bond Street, the fine shop still occupied, which, later that century, was spread to Nos. 165 to 169, and to 22 Albemarle Street. He was soon producing from his workshop on the premises the best dressing and writing cases money could buy, as well as other fine items of leather-work and jewellery. With this fame and success, Queen Victoria bestowed her Royal Warrant in 1861, and since then Asprey's have served every reigning monarch.

Today the firm, now famous around the world, maintains its standards of impeccable workmanship and the courteous belief that every whim of a customer can and must be fulfilled. Its unique feature in a modern world of standardisation is that exquisite and often highly individualistic articles – destined for the dazzling showrooms or special customers – are still designed and made in their own "factory" above the Bond Street showrooms. Its products may include anything from a golden folding toothbrush to a four-foot replica of Concorde in silver (the latter displayed in the shop and sold within two days). Today Asprey's, with its many departments dealing in fine gold and silver, in glass and china, in leather goods and antique furniture, has maintained unbroken its remarkable tradition of family ownership: the business has never failed to pass from father to son.

The famous old firm of silversmiths and jewellers, Tessiers, occupy one

The high and exceptionally grand entrance of Asprey's at 165–9 New Bond Street, considered an important example of the new Victorian type of iron and plate-glass shop-front

The solid, and also very fine, front of Tessiers at 26 New Bond Street

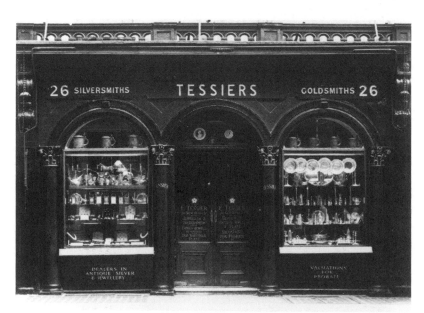

of New Bond Street's original houses at No. 26, a building which is considerably smaller than its neighbours. Built as a private house early in the eighteenth century, it did not become a shop until about 1840, when it was occupied by Winfield & Sims who sold military beds and camp equipment. Tessiers themselves have occupied it since 1852, and its attractive Victorian shop-front can have changed little since those days.

The Tessier family were French Huguenots, descended from Etienne de Teissier, who arrived in England as a refugee in 1712. His grandson Lewis, who simplified the spelling of his surname, was a jewellery merchant who helped many French *émigrés* to dispose of their valuables. By the time of Lewis's death in 1811, his son already had three retail jewellery businesses in Mayfair, and in the middle of that century 26 New Bond Street was also acquired, at an annual rent of £7 14s, and they set up here as jewellers with a "Specialité for Onyx and Mourning Jewellery", and "Artists in Hair". Until 1877 the business was in the hands of Tessier descendants. The lease of 26 New Bond Street then passed to a Mr Henderson and, in 1882, to John Vander and John Hedges. In 1900 it was acquired by the two brothers Arthur and Frank Parsons and descendants of this family continue in the business to the present day.

In addition to Asprey and Tessier, Philip Antrobus continues Bond Street's proud tradition of jewellers: established in 1815, they moved to Old Bond Street in 1949, and are now at 11 New Bond Street. It was in their workshop here that the engagement ring for Her Majesty Queen Elizabeth II was produced. These Georgian premises are also renowned as having once housed Charles Dickens for a few weeks when he stayed in Bond Street to research an article he had been commissioned to write for the *London Journal* on the arcades of Bond Street and the adjoining area.

And then, of course, there is Cartier's at 175 New Bond Street, in large Victorian premises on the site of the grand old Clarendon Hotel.

117

It was back in 1849 that the firm was first established in Paris by Louis Francois Cartier, where it won such a glamorous reputation that the future Edward VII himself suggested to Cartier's grandson that he also establish himself in London, in association with Jean and Gaston Worth. This was done in 1900, and in 1909 Cartier's moved to 175 New Bond Street, under the direction of Jacques Cartier, who designed his own jewellery, opening a workshop in 1921. Today a fabulous range of Cartier jewellery is designed and made on the upper floors of the Bond Street premises. It is a dazzling array of beautiful objects such as have always made Cartier's famous, though it includes also items for more modest tastes and purses, suiting a wider public, and some of the world's finest hand-made watches.

The chemists Savory & Moore were established at 143 New Bond Street in 1797. Their beautiful Georgian shop-front, displaying the Royal Warrant of Queen Victoria, still stands, though the premises were rebuilt in 1957. The original building was a fine example of the work of George Maddox, an estimable architect who specialised in pharmacies and after whom Maddox Street (which crosses Bond Street nearby) was named. The floor boards of the old pharmacy were said to have come from the original Drury Lane stage.

In October 1957 John Betjeman, who feared the worst from signs of rebuilding, wrote to the *Spectator:* "A good piece of news comes from Bond Street, where I have for some time looked with apprehension at Number 143, where there is a notice of demolition. This building contains the charming chemist's shop of Savory and Moore with its square panes and iron railings and late Georgian interior complete with jars and mahogany shelves and paintings of herbs. . . . The Savory family lived above the shop in Bond Street in the eighteenth century and their descendant Mr D. A. Savory tells me that his firm is going to some trouble and no little expense in retaining the old shop front and its interior in the new building that is to go up on the site."

The apothecary Thomas Savory had been a Gentleman of the

King's Privy Chamber, and had entertained lavishly in his fine apartments above the shop. His dinner guests included doctors from Savile Row (then the doctors' quarter), the Duke of Cambridge, a close friend and frequent visitor, who played the fiddle with Savory, and the Duke of Sussex, brother of the Prince Regent.

Thomas was followed by his stolid nephew John Savory, a founder member of the Pharmaceutical Society who for many years edited the *Savory Compendium to Modern Medicine*. The most profitable ventures of Savory & Moore in these early days were the original patented Seidlitz Powders and the digestive lozenges of Dr Jenner, the great pioneer against smallpox. The latter were in fact still on sale in Bond Street in 1938. Famous patrons, in addition to members of the royal family, included the Duke of Wellington, Emma Lady Hamilton and Florence Nightingale: indeed for a time Savory & Moore profited much from her uncovering of scandalous hospital conditions as theirs was the valuable contract for sending medical supplies to the Crimea. When this lucrative adventure ended another was at hand with the production of Savory & Moore's famous artificial baby food, which brought international fame.

Up till the end of the First World War all Savory & Moore's products were manufactured in their own factory adjacent to their Bond Street premises; later this was moved to Tottenham. Today the company, expanded by mergers, continues it sturdy traditions, still looking out from its picturesque old shop-front and proudly serving members of the royal family.

The growth of the worldwide Elizabeth Arden empire, with treatment salons in most of the world's capitals and laboratories in fourteen countries, is one of the great success stories of this century. Behind it stood the petite, pretty Canadian-born Florence Nightingale Graham, whose feminine delicacy in appearance and manner belied her single-minded strength and business acumen. After gaining some initial experience in a small beauty salon in New York, she launched her own

The attractive Georgian shop-front of Savory & Moore, preserved when these premises at 143 New Bond Street were rebuilt

Yardley's original Bond Street shop at 8 Old Bond Street, opened in
1910

talents on the ripe beauty product market, formulating a new complete method of skin care and, under the name of Elizabeth Arden, opening her own salon on Fifth Avenue – which was soon to proliferate into every major American city. In 1922 a London Salon was opened in Bond Street – to be followed by others right round the world, while Elizabeth Arden herself continued to superintend her vast international enterprise in painstaking detail, personally testing and approving each new product.

Elizabeth Arden preparations were at first manufactured above the London Salon at 25 Old Bond Street, a fine Georgian building of particular architectural interest which is now occupied at street level by the well-known silversmiths Mappin & Webb. With the expansion of the business, however, the Elizabeth Arden "factory" moved from Bond Street. Today the organisation has been taken under the wing of the great American pharmaceutical company Eli Lilly, but London is still the largest manufacturing centre for Elizabeth Arden products outside the United States, and it exports to many countries. In 1970 the Elizabeth Arden Salon opened in new premises at 20 New Bond Street, where "in a warm, relaxing atmosphere may be found everything needed for top to toe beauty" as well as "fashion for all occasions".

Yardley & Company Limited, whose head office is at 33 Old Bond Street (at the corner of Stafford Street), is today part of a worldwide cosmetics group owned by British American Tobacco. Its small beginnings were in a little soap and perfumery business founded in the City in 1770 and known first as Cleavers. Later the business passed to William Yardley, father-in-law of the founder's son, but it remained small compared to other soap manufacturers of the time.

A rise in fortunes was engineered by the energetic management of the brothers Thornton and Richard Gardner, who removed to premises at 8 New Bond Street in the early years of the twentieth century. With sophisticated marketing techniques (including the adoption as its trademark for lavender products – of which Yardley was soon to be the foremost producer in the world – of Francis Wheatley's now famous Flower-Sellers Group) they moved fully into the public eye.

Since those days the House of Yardley has never looked back. By the 1930s cosmetics had become respectable, and methods of mass production had put them within the reach of every woman. Today nearly one thousand cosmetic lines for both sexes are exported to one hundred and thirty countries around the world. The international business of Yardley & Company Limited is still directed from the Old Bond Street headquarters, where there is also a trade showroom and a beauty salon which is open to the public.

Truefitt & Hill, "Hair Artists since 1805", are at 23 Old Bond Street. They have never been far from this site: late in the nineteenth century they shared the premises at No. 13 with Benson & Hedges, moving later to No. 16, and in the beginning, in 1805, it was at No. 40 that Francis Truefitt first set himself up as a Court hair cutter and head dresser. Truefitt's are mentioned in Thackeray's *The Four Georges* as wigmakers to George IV. The clientele has always been of both sexes (one famous twentieth-century male regular being Field-Marshal Viscount Montgomery), although, when Truefitt's were first established, only fashionable men would have entered their doors to have their meticulous hairstyles carefully dressed. Feminine artifices were produced only in the secrecy of their own homes: a fashionable lady could not have been seen to need improvement. For a special occasion she would have summoned her hairdresser to her house; she would not have gone to him. This was all to change, however, and Truefitt's themselves, who offered their services with the utmost refinement, did much to change it.

The "Shirt Makers, Hosiers & Outfitters" Beale & Inman at 131–2 New Bond Street have been established now for one hundred and fifty years: it was in 1828 that James Beale opened a gentlemen's hosiery business here. A few years later he took into partnership Richard Inman, who, through diligent travels on the Continent, established a valuable export trade, winning the patronage of royal heads of Europe, among them the King of the Netherlands and Napoleon III. Today the export of quality merchandise is continued, though now to the richer pastures of North America. Famous customers at home, in addition to members of the British royal family, have included Charles Dickens and, more recently, Winston Churchill. Today the Governing Director of the firm is Mr Victor Inman, grandson of Richard Inman: it is interesting to find yet another proud family tradition maintained in Bond Street.

W. Bill Limited, the famous woollen merchants, are unique in having premises both at 93 New Bond Street, opened in 1910, and 28 Old Bond Street, opened in the 1960s. The Old Bond Street premises were acquired after an unsuccessful attempt at opening in Jermyn Street convinced them, in the words of Mr David Bill, Chairman, that "we needed to be in a street which attracted the overseas visitors who form the largest part of our business". The second Bond Street shop "proved to be a very good move" and, interestingly, "did not take away any of the business from the shop at the other end of the street."

This family business was founded by William Bill in 1846 in Mold, Wales, from where it expanded to Tenby and then, in 1892, to London, reaching Bond Street in 1910.

Today the firm, still run by descendants of William Bill, continues to offer the best in pure woollen goods, and it has been nominated by the Association of National Retail Merchants of the United States as "One of the Great Shops of Europe". One of its most interesting claims to fame is that it was W. Bill Limited who supplied their special light-weight Shetland pullovers to Sir Ernest Shackleton for the Antarctic, and to leaders of the successful Everest expedition of 1953, as well as to numerous other expeditions.

The last word in feminine elegance, Fenwick's of 63 New Bond Street, had its origins in the small shop opened in Newcastle in 1882 by John James Fenwick, whose aim was to offer his clients a new range of ladies' fashions of a character and style entirely his own. This enterprise succeeded to such an extent that in 1891 he was able to open his doors to London's elite in the heart of prosperous Bond Street. It was a bold step, but from the beginning an immensely successful one: famous patrons from royalty downwards soon helped to build up his remarkable reputation. In 1930 the premises were greatly enlarged by the addition of the adjoining Rover House and today Fenwick's can claim to be Bond Street's only department store. J. J. Fenwick himself died in 1905, but subsequent generations were left to continue the proud tradition he had set.

The White House, Bond Street's world-renowned linen specialists, have been established at 51 New Bond Street since 1906, though their present fine building is the result of extensive alterations made in 1930. It houses spacious halls of the finest linens, lingerie and fashion and children's wear, many items of which are made in workrooms on the premises. The showrooms of The White House are unusual in all being on the ground floor, and enjoying natural daylight.

At 24 Old Bond Street is the firm of Salvatore Ferragamo, makers of the finest quality shoes and accessories and a fine selection of ready-to-wear fashions. Earlier, between 1952 and 1968, they were established at No. 18.

The story of the firm's founder, Salvatore Ferragamo, is one of a fairy-tale rise to fame which is told in his autobiography *Shoemaker of Dreams*. One of a very large but not wealthy family, he was, unusually, obsessed with shoemaking from childhood, actually opening his own shop at the age of eleven in his home village near Naples. At fourteen he set off for the promised land of America and there prospered magnificently: he was soon making shoes for the fashionable rich and many Hollywood stars. Established and wealthy, he returned to Italy in 1927, but times were soon to become bad and his business ventures at first sunk him into poverty. But he did not give up: within another four years he was not only on his feet again but had acquired the prestigious thirteenth-century Palazzo Feroni in Florence which is still the headquarters of the firm. In the following years his fortune was consolidated, and today members of his family continue his masterly devotion to his craft.

The firm of H. & M. Rayne, "Makers of exclusive footwear", at 15 and 16 Old Bond Street was founded in 1889 by Henry and Mary Rayne (grandparents of the present Chairman and Managing Director, Edward Rayne) as theatrical costumiers in Waterloo Road. Among their more famous early customers were Dame Madge Kendall, Lily Langtry, Marie Tempest, Evelyn Laye, Jessie Matthews and George Edwardes. From the beginning they also supplied boots and shoes to go with the costumes they made, and by the turn of the century the footwear side of the business had extended to ladies' shoes for ordinary wear, custom made for many famous actresses of the day.

After the First World War, Rayne opened a shoe shop at 58 New Bond Street, bringing their exclusive lines in ladies' day and evening shoes to a wider market. It proved an immediate success. Soon they were supplying members of the royal family. The Royal Warrant was granted to them by Queen Mary – an honour to be repeated by Queen Elizabeth, the Queen Mother, and our present Queen. In 1936 the premises at 16 Old Bond Street were acquired, in conjunction with Herman Delman of the United States. Today, in addition to a large export trade, Rayne have three London shops and many "shops within shops" all over the country. Since 1973 they have been part of Debenhams Limited, and through other subsidiaries have acquired many retail outlets in the United States: Rayne are today the leading American retailers of quality shoes.

Henry Maxwell & Company, "Makers of boots, shoes, spurs, whips and leather goods", were founded in 1750 in Worcester, moving soon afterwards to Soho. Though they have been at 177 New Bond Street only since 1973, they were for many years at nearby premises in Dover Street, and, before that, in Piccadilly. Their founder Henry Maxwell was a spur maker of good repute, and until the early twentieth century Maxwell's made only spurs; subsequently the boot and shoe side of the business was developed. In 1974 Maxwell's were appointed as boot-makers to Her Majesty Queen Elizabeth II, which means that they have been Royal Warrant-holders since the days of George IV.

Today Maxwell's are one of a group of companies headed by H. Huntsman & Sons, the old-established Tailors and Breeches Makers of 11 Savile Row, who themselves had a long connection with Bond Street, having occupied premises at 125 New Bond Street between 1814 and about 1890. Two other companies in the group also have long-standing connections with the street. Rowes of Bond Street, manufacturers of children's wear, have been at 120 New Bond Street since Victorian times, having started out at Gosport as tailors to the Royal Navy. When Queen Victoria chose to dress her children in little naval uniforms, it was Rowes who were commissioned to make them. This soon set a fashion for the offspring of the aristocracy and other royal families of Europe, and Rowes set up in Bond Street to cater for this new trade in sailor suits. The second firm is H. W. Brettell, the shirtmakers, who have been in the Royal Arcade since their foundation in 1880. It was Queen Victoria's patronage of Brettell's which, as mentioned earlier, earned the important prefix of "Royal" for the new Arcade off Old Bond Street.

At 127 New Bond Street is the photographers' paradise which is the headquarters of Wallace Heaton Limited. In the year that Fox Talbot first revealed his method of making photographs, 1839, a Mr Wreaks opened a chemist shop in Sheffield which was later sold to Messrs Watson & Norris. Mr Norris soon took up this new idea of photography and before long the little shop called Watson's was sporting a comprehensive and expanding photographic section. In 1902 Wallace Evans Heaton, a young pharmaceutical chemist who had also interested himself in photography, took over the business and greatly expanded the photographic side through advertising in *Amateur Photographer* –

advertising which has been continued ever since. In 1914 Wallace Heaton became a founder member of the Photographic Dealers' Association and for twelve years was its Hon. Secretary; in 1920 he was elected President. During the First World War the company became official photographic printers to the Admiralty, and ever since have been contractors to the Government. In 1918 the name of the company was changed to Wallace Heaton Limited and in the following year, by which time several additional premises had been acquired, the bold step of moving up to 119 New Bond Street ("right in the heart of the fashion and cosmetic houses and antique dealers") was taken. Contrary to some gloomy prognostications the business soon flourished here. In those early days the Bond Street shop was managed by a Mr Banning, with two girl assistants, while a Mr Hardwick ran the developing and printing side in the basement, where he processed some thirty films a day by hand – a practice continued on the premises until 1920, when special developing and printing premises were needed in London as the business had expanded considerably. In 1932 Wallace Heaton Limited received the Royal Warrant; by 1936 the organisation had grown vastly and in that year the headquarters was moved from 119 to 127 New Bond Street, where it remains. In later years the adjoining premises at No. 126 were also acquired.

Early twentieth-century lists of Bond Street's firms show the sudden popularity of the society photographer. In 1911 there were as many as fourteen photographic studios, though in 1886, in addition to the Amateur Photographic Association, there are only four. One of these is of particular interest: the studio of William Friese-Greene (1855–1921), the inventor of cinematography (and the subject of a film starring Robert Donat).

Early in 1885 Friese-Greene, who already had portrait studios in Bath, Bristol and Plymouth, arrived in London determined to set himself up in the West End, though he had only £200 for rent and equipment. Going into partnership with Esmé Collins, who was able to put up a similar amount of money, they opened a studio at 69 New Bond Street, in two rooms above a shoe shop. Their young receptionist Winifred Tagg, who was just fifteen when first employed, left her impressions of the establishment and the handsome, amiable Friese-Greene and his more earnest partner. It surprised her that such nice gentlemen should be content with such meagre and shabby accommodation. The studio, at the top of narrow, dark stairs, was carpeted with ragged oilcloth, while its cold, dark little dressing-room was inelegantly and sparsely furnished with an ancient horse-hair sofa and dressing-table. To this incongruously mean setting came a splendid array of titled people and society ladies – even "ladies from Queen Victoria's drawing-room" resplendent in fine gowns, feathers and veils.

Friese-Greene, as even Winifred could see, was not much of a businessman: he began spending an increasing amount of time away from the studio, and quarrels with Esmé Collins were frequent. Nevertheless, despite his preoccupation with motion picture experiments, he eventually acquired eight London studios and one in Brighton, but it was not long before the Bond Street studio was taken over by his partner as Friese-Greene faced bankruptcy. Much later he died virtually penniless, but in dramatic circumstances, minutes after the shabby old man had addressed a stormy meeting of the cinema trade, to most of whom he was quite unknown.

Benson & Hedges, "a firm established in the Old Bond Street of a more leisured age, which invested the craft of cigarette making with an accomplished artistry, adding lustre to the joys of smoking" is at No. 13. The foundations of the business were laid in 1873 by Richard Benson and William Hedges at these very premises, where once Gentleman Jackson had taught the classic arts of boxing and fencing to the nobility and gentry. In the early days the premises were shared with Truefitt's the famous Court hairdressers. After twelve years Benson severed his connection with the business, which became the responsi-

128

A reconstruction of the original Benson & Hedges shop at 13
Old Bond Street, in Victorian times

129

bility of William Hedges and, later, of his son Alfred, who in turn was followed by a third generation.

In the early days of ready-made cigarettes great services indeed were paid to the smoking world by Edward VII, under whose fashionable leadership smoking became socially acceptable. It was at his special request that Benson & Hedges first produced a new cigarette from Egyptian tobacco which soon earned widespread approbation under the name of "Cairo Citadel". Benson & Hedges have been awarded several Royal Warrants, the first, surprisingly enough, from Queen Victoria, despite her abhorrence of smoking.

For Benson & Hedges, as for so many old firms, the twentieth century has brought accelerating growth. Even in the early years of the century there were big changes at 13 Old Bond Street. Space previously occupied by Truefitt's was turned over to cigarette manufacture until, after the First World War, this activity was removed to Fulham and the Bond Street premises were left as a "quiet, dignified and unpretentious" showroom. The demand for Virginia instead of Turkish tobacco now increased, and the popularity of cigarette smoking continued to grow. During the Second World War 13 Old Bond Street was bombed and a vast stock of cigarettes and cigars was lost through ensuing fire. Recovery was swift, however, and Benson & Hedges emerged at the end of the war with a name which stood higher than ever before in the popular esteem, and one which had spread far beyond the shores of Britain.

Fine old firms Bond Street has in plenty, and some not so old which nevertheless are worthy inheritors of a famous mantel. For one there is the Ireland House Shop at 150 New Bond Street, opened in 1966 in conjunction with the Irish Government, but now independent, and selling the best of Irish merchandise of every sort: Waterford crystal, Beleek china, fashion dresses and knitwear and coats, Irish linen. . . . For another there is the little fashion mecca, Robina, at 174 New Bond Street, "the brainchild of Robina Ziff, a young lady who seeks the ultimate in perfection" – a choice old Bond Street ideal indeed. Her clothes "are in the modern idiom, but without being extreme, so that women of all ages and nationalities can be beautifully dressed and retain an air of grace and movement" . . . And there are others.

Of the famous firms who have moved from Bond Street in recent years perhaps the most notable was Scotts, the hatters, who occupied the prestigious address of No. 1 Old Bond Street, on the corner of Piccadilly, for about a century, although in fact hats were sold there as early as 1758. For long their smart turn-out, the horse-drawn vermilion van with a top-hatted coachman, was a famous feature in West End traffic. Today Scotts are established nearby in St James's Street.

Another familiar presence in Bond Street until recently was of the world-famous tailors Gieves, now Gieves & Hawkes of 1 Savile Row. The grand old firm of naval tailors and outfitters, Gieves, whose history goes back nearly two hundred years, began with the shop which was opened by Melchizdeck Meredith, grandfather of the novelist George Meredith (who immortalised him as "Old Mel" in *Evan Harrington*) in Portsmouth in 1784, where it fitted out many an early midshipman and captain. As the business grew in importance many other shops were opened, including one at 27 Old Bond Street, within sight of the new Gieves & Hawkes Savile Row premises. The even older firm of Hawkes had been founded in 1771 as tailors to the army – including the Duke of Wellington. "Both firms", their amalgamated successor tells us, "prospered through the Service connection, despite the fact that in those days it was scarcely done for a gentleman to settle his tailor's bill" – in 1938 it was calculated that the Royal Navy owed Gieves almost £500,000 in unpaid debts accumulated in the days when money really was money!

There is a fine story to the effect that Charles Laughton, before making "Mutiny on the Bounty", which he hoped would be as pains-takingly authentic as possible, called at the Bond Street shop, asking:

"I wish to enquire about some uniforms you made some time ago for Captain William Bligh."

"When were they made, sir?" queried the well-drilled clerk.

"About 1789."

"Yes, sir." He disappeared and promptly returned with an ancient leather-bound order book listing all the required specifications, which were carefully noted and meticulously reproduced in the film, to the approval of even Gieves themselves.

Unhappily, during the bombing raids of the Second World War such old records were destroyed – a sad loss indeed of fascinating lists of illustrious names, including no less a sailor than Nelson himself.

Bond Street was once famous for its hotels – and it is still renowned for one, the Westbury, at the corner of Conduit Street and New Bond Street. Though, on the outside, it is dismissed by Pevsner as "a dull, efficient-looking modern block", it is indeed "a luxury hotel with a worldwide reputation for friendly service and excellent cuisine." Since 1977 a part of the Trust Houses Forte group, the Westbury was, when it arose two decades previously, the first hotel to be built in the West End for a quarter of a century, and also the first in Britain to be operated by an American company, the Knott Hotels Corporation, the oldest hotel chain in the United States. The Westbury was opened by the American Ambassador on March 1st, 1955 – which begins to seem a long while ago when one recalls that a single room then cost £3 10s nightly. The hotel's cocktail lounge is of particular interest, having been transformed some years ago into an "eighteenth-century" library called "The Tenison Room" after Dr Thomas Tenison, an Archbishop of Canterbury whose chapel, Trinity Chapel, used to stand in Conduit Street, on part of the site of the Westbury, until replaced by shops in 1877.

These pages must not end without a tribute to the Bond Street Association. Formed in 1924 by a group of Bond Street Directors, it is "a non-profitmaking body through which rare complaints are channelled, ideas for improvement exchanged and implemented and liaison is maintained with official bodies such as the Westminster City Council and various Ministries". It deals with all the thorny problems which arise in regard to traffic congestion (in fact the main reason for its formation in 1924 was the need for traffic control), maintenance (including the protection of the general appearance of the neighbourhood) and trading policies. If such matters sound mundane, not so its real aims, which are "to preserve and enhance Bond Street's renown for fashion and exclusive merchandise. . . . It ensures that Bond Street's reputation is respected and admired throughout the world. . . . The pursuit of elegance, excellence and the high standards of service to customers maintained by the older houses and accepted by the newest, is the aim of all members of the Association." On what more encouraging note to end a eulogy on the "street of London's charms the centre"?

THE INHABITANTS OF BOND STREET

* * *

In 1811

From Boyle's *Court and Country Guide and Town Visiting Directory*,
corrected up to January 1st, 1811

OLD BOND STREET

11 Hebb, Wm.
13 Slade, F. Moore
14 Pope, Alexander
17 Spence, Geo., Dentist to the King
21 M'Clary, Jas.
25 Pybus, Call, Martin, & Hale, Messrs., Bankers
30 Grimstone, Hon. Mrs.
36 Elizee, P., Surgeon

NEW BOND STREET

1 Wildman, William
18 Royal, Major
29 Town, Benjamin
47 Prickett, Geo.
61 Archer, Rev. James
69 Campbell, William
112 Schipper, G.
143 Katalani, Mad.
154 Picton, Gen. W.
156 Mackett, Charles
160 Birch and Chambers
162 Stewart, Wm. C.
Staveley, Lieut.-Gen.
Cooke, Col.
171 Hutchins, Wm.
172 Stump, John
168 Harris, Wm.

In 1840

From Tallis's *London Street Views*, 1840

OLD BOND STREET

1 Moore & Co., Army Accoutrement Manufacturers
2 Griffiths, Thomas, Hatter
3 Falkner, Music Seller and Publisher
4 Poulton, George, Fishmonger
5 Starkey, Gold and Silver Laceman
6 Lloyd & Co., Hosiers, Glovers, and Shirtmakers
7 Gayford, Chesterford, Wine and Spirit Merchant
8 Webb, John, Upholsterer and Cabinet Maker
9 Bowman, Frederick, Dealer in Bramah's Locks, Pens, and Manufacturer of Desks and Dressing Cases, &c.
10 Marshall, J. H., Wine and Spirit Merchant
Here Western Exchange
11 Cape, George Augustus, Tailor
12 Edge, Thomas, Lamp and Chandelier Manufacturer

135

12 Pons, Madame, Milliner, &c.
13 Gilbert & Goatley, Bootmakers
13 Yates, Picture Dealer
14 Carpenter, James, Bookseller and Publisher
15 Hookham, Thomas, Bookseller and Librarian
16 Higgins & Son, Hosiers, Glovers, and Shirtmakers
17 Lyle, J., Purveyor of Coffee to the Royal Family
17 Smallwood, E., Alexandrian Institution, New Public Subscription British and Foreign Literary Association
18 Wilson, Wellman & Wilson, Tailors
19, 20 Lapworth & Riley, Carpet Manufacturers to Her Majesty and the Royal Family

Here Meade's Court

21 Stanley, George, Auctioneer
22 Tinkler & Co., Silk Mercers and Lacemen
23 Webb, Charles, Gold and Silver Laceman
24 Atkinson, James & Edward, Wholesale and Retail Perfumers

Here Burlington Gardens

25 Call (Sir W. P., Bart.), Martin & Co., Bankers
26 Lonsdale, Christopher, Music Library

27 Ebers & Co., Booksellers and Librarians
28 Brooks & Hedger, Surveyors and Land Agents
29 Tossell (late Cracknell), Breeches Maker
30 Chapman & Moore, Hatters to the Queen
31 Binnie & Richardson, Tailors
32 Mansfield, Charles, Wine and Spirit Merchant
33 Mitchell, John, Bookseller and Publisher

Here Stafford Street

34 Bloor & Co., China Manufacturers
35 Watson, Wood & Bell, Carpet and Rug Manufacturers
36 Soloman, E., Optician
36 Charden, A., Perfumer
37 Bullock, B. H., Wine Merchant
37 Weston & Sprague, Tailors
39 Wallace, Thomas, Butcher
40 Steward, Purveyor of Milk and Cream
40 Hood, Thomas, Hatter
41 Smyth, Surgeon
41 Richardson, John, Cheesemonger
42 Andrews, Samuel, Tea and Coffee Dealer
43 Powell & Co., Coach Builders
44 Whitfield (late Cullum), Butterman
45 Othen, Venison Dealer
46 Simpson, Bread and Biscuit Baker

Here Piccadilly

NEW BOND STREET

1 Truefitt, Francis, by Special Appointment, Perfumer and Court Head Dresser to Her Majesty
2 Capon, William, Hatter
3 Dixey, G. & C., Opticians to the Queen
4 Hay, John, Tailor
5 Walker, J., & Co., Tailors and Breeches Makers to Her Majesty's Household
6 Isherwood, John, Decorator and Upholsterer
7 Roberts, Keturah, Perfumer
8 Styles, Henry Thomas, Tobacconist
8 Sherrard, Surgeon
9 Brookes, Book and Print Publisher
9 Lawrence, George, Dressing Case Maker
10 Grierson, Charles, Gunmaker
11 Hillhouse, Charles, Hosier, Hatter, and Glover

12 Hillhouse, M., Child Bed Linen Warehouse
13 Harrison, John, Bootmaker
13 Smith, Ann, Milliner
13 Woollatt, Dealer in Curiosities
14 Reynauld, J. B., Silk Mercer
15 Allcroft, Music Seller
16 Long's Hotel, Markwell, W. J., Wine Merchant; and at No. 11, Grafton Street

Here Clifford Street

17 Hancock, Thomas, Goldsmith and Jeweller
18 Scott, G. & C., Wine Merchants (Stevens's Hotel)
19 Saunderson, Joseph, Tailor
20 Redmayne, Giles, Silk Mercer
21 Grieve, William, Ladies' Shoe Manufacturer

22 Cooper, T., Umbrella and Parasol Manufacturer
23 Dr. Culverwell's Bathing Establishment
23 Cooper, James, Tailor and Mercer
23 Ince, Thomas, Wine Merchant
23 Watton, G. H., Tobacconist
Here Conduit Street
24 Cadbury & Son, Buttermen and Cheesemongers
25 Thompson, Adam, Watch and Clock Maker
26 Winfield & Sims, Camp Equipage Warehouse, R. N. Hayes, Agent
27 Bann, Boot Maker
28 Mori & Lavenu, Music Sellers
29 Boone, Bookseller
30 Charters & Co., Coach and Harness Makers
31 Allason, Bookseller and Stationer
32 Hook, J., Ladies' Shoe Maker
33 Dollman, Boot Maker
34 Cripps, T., Black Horse Yard
35 Rigge, Brockbank & Rigge, Perfumers to the Royal Family
36 Kirby, Thomas, Oilman and Fish Sauce Warehouse
37 Edlin, Toy Warehouse and Fancy Brush Maker
38 Wand, C., Pastry Cook to the Queen
39 Adam & Co., Fruiterers
40 Mavor, Veterinary Surgeon
41 Oliver, Charles, Music Seller
42 Allen, Tailor
43 Richardson, Cutler and Dressing Case Manufacturer
44 Hedges & Son, Boot Makers
45 Page, Ladies' Shoe Maker
46 Rodwell, Bookseller
Here Maddox Street
47 Pratt, S. and T., Importers of Antique Furniture, Armour, &c.
48 Brewster, Peruke Maker and Perfumer to the Royal Family
49 Kennedy, Stationer and Dressing Case Maker
50 Chappell, Music Seller to Her Majesty
51 Haines, Poulterer
52 Clarke, H., Linen Draper
53 Duggin, Hat Maker
54 Guthrie & Son, Tailors

55 Hugh, James, Tailor
56 Rimmell, Licensed to Let Horses for Hire
57 Gattie and Pierce, Perfumers
58, 59 Turners, Goldsmiths to the Royal Family
60 Williams, W., Hatter
61 Brooker & Dollman, Booksellers
62 Perigal & Dutterneau, Watch and Clock Makers
63 Frazer & Wood, Oilmen, &c.
Here Little Brook Street
64 Ange, L., Watch Maker
65 Lahee, Estate and Auction Office
66 Buckland, Silk Mercers
67 Johnstone, Jupe & Co., Patentees of the Circular Dining Tables
68 Taylor, George, Tailor
69 Egley, Bookseller
70 Barnes, Hatter and East India Warehouse
71 Blount, Arnold, Silk Mercer
72 Perry, G. & Co., Lustre Makers to the Queen
73 Phillips, Auctioneer
74 Huntly, Seal and Copper Plate Engraver
75 Tarner, Thomas, Stationer, &c.
Here Union Street
76 Fisher, Chemist and Druggist
77 Owen, Fruiterer and Purveyor to Her Majesty
78 Tomlinson & Co., Shirt Makers
79 Hook, Hatter
80 Arrowsmith, H. W. & A. (late Henderson), Decorators, Upholsterers, and Gilders to Her Majesty
— Smith, Mr. H. S., Artist
81 Ball & Son, Oilmen, &c.
82 Potter, Silk Mercer
83 Pauli, Furrier
84 Dann, Johnson & Co., Teamen and Grocers
85 Clement & Co., Depôt des Modes
86 Boyer, Pearl Wax Light Depôt
Here Oxford Street
87 Marks, P., & Co., Fruiterers
88 Morant, G., & Son, Interior Decorators
89 Mayhew & White, Hat Manufacturers
90 Jarratt & Woodhouse, Hatters
91 Hodgkinson & Co., Linen Drapers
92 Hoadley, Carriage Builder

93 Wells, Tailor, &c.
94 Blenheim Hotel, John Bennett
  Here Blenheim Street
95 Owen, India Shawl Warehouse
96 Boyd, A., Furnishing Ironmonger
97 Davis & Son, Wine and Brandy Merchants
98 Burnand, G. C., Carriage Builder
99 Turner & Shepherd, Seedsmen and Florists
100 Strachan, Saddler and Harness Maker
101 Green Man Tavern, John Chorley Clarke
102 Keene, C., & Co., Drapers and Hosiers
103 Emanuel and Town, Manufacturers of Buhl to Her Majesty
104 Francis, Upholsterer and Cabinet Maker
105 Summers, Manufacturer of Stoves, &c.
106 Kingsbury, Cutler and Dressing Case Maker
107 Hardwick & Son, Silk Mercers
108 Halstead, Bookseller and Stationer
108 Basil, Wood, Wine Merchant
109 Challoner, Laceman
110 Giblett, W., Butcher, Purveyor to Her Majesty
  Here Brook Street
111 Baker, H., & Co., Hosiers, &c.
112 Furnis & Son, Hatters and Silk Mercers
113 Cooper & Batchelor, Linen Drapers
114 Dickinson, Publisher and Print Seller
115 Scaife, A., & Co., Tailors and Habit Makers
116, 117 Smyths, Perfumers
118
119 Szarka, F., & Co., Furriers
120 Griffith & Pearson, Tailors
121 Kenneth, J., Fishmonger
122 Hodges, Wine and Spirit Vaults
  Here Lancashire Court
123 Pratt, S. & H., Trunk and Camp Equipage Warehouse
124 Hudson & Falconer, Tailors
125 Milne, Carriage Builder
126 Preston & Son, Tailors
127 Andre, Hatter
128 Fletcher, H. & C., Military Tailors
129 Daniel, China and Glass Warehouse
  Here Grosvenor Street
130 Rateau & Co., Dyers and Scourers
130 Corr, J., Boot and Shoe Maker

131 Beale, Shirt Maker, &c.
132 Brown, Italian Warehouse
133 Brockell & Son, Shirt Makers
134 Evans, R. & J. E., Grocers
135 Amor, John, Wine and Brandy Merchant
136 Moore, J., Breeches Maker
137 Smith & Sons, Carvers and Gilders
  Henry Sadler's Livery Stables
138 Smethurst, Lamp Manufacturer
139 Turner, Appraiser and Cabinet Maker
140 Mills, R., Musical Circulating Library
141 Dean, Boot and Shoe Maker
142 Spain & Cork, Coach Makers
143 Savory & Moore, Chemists to the Royal Family
144 Thornhill, Cutler to Her Majesty
145 Fearon, H. B., Wine Merchant
146 Duer, Bread and Biscuit Baker
147 Glenton & Chapman, Furnishing Ironmongers, &c.
148 Hart, Embroidery Dépôt
149 Lambe, A. B., Mineral Water Warehouse
150 Grove, John & Christopher, Fishmongers
151 Lancaster, Charles, Gun Maker
152 Osmond & Simpson, Woollen Drapers
  Here Bruton Street
153 Thomas, F. L., & J. W., Goldsmiths and Jewellers
154 Merrington & Co., Linen Drapers
155 Chamberlain, Walter & Co., Worcester Porcelain Manufacturers
156 Storr & Mortimer, Jewellers and Silversmiths
157 Jarvis, Mademoiselle, Milliner
157 Storey & Robinson, Tailors
158 Delcroix & Co., Perfumers
158 Duchoy, Madame
159 Wilson, John, & Sons, Linen Warehouse
160 Royal Naval Club
161 Hughton, W., Stationer, Bookseller, Newsagent, and Writing Case Manufacturer
162 Bertram & Son, Wine Merchants
163 Payne, W., Watch and Clock Maker
164 Kent & Bull, Linen Drapers and Warehousemen
165 Barnes, John, Wig Maker and Hair Cutter
165 Warne, Thomas, Antigropelo **Manu**facturer

166 Baldry, W. C., Mercer and Woollen Draper
167 Andrews, Bookseller, Stationer, and Librarian
168 Barnett, T., Esq.
169 Chaplain, Mrs., Carendon Hotel
170 Bishop, W., Gold and Silversmith, and Agent to Westley Richards, Gun Manufacturer
171 Fraser, Branwell & Co., Tailors
172 Dinneford, Charles, Chemist and Druggist

In 1886

From *Post Office London Street Directory*, 1886

OLD BOND STREET

1 Scott & Co., Silk and Felt Hats, Caps, &c. of Christy's manufacture
Laurance, Henry, Oculist Optician
1a Deschamps, Chas. Wm., Picture Dealer
2 Greger, Max, Limited, Wine Merchants
3 & 4 Hill Brothers, Military Tailors
6 Hummel, E. & H., & Co., Hosiers
M'Neill, Maj.-Gen. Sir John Carstairs, K.C.B., K.C.M.G. and V.C.
7 Gayford & Co., Wine Merchants
Hansard, Henry L.
8 Wilkinson & Son, Upholsterers
9 Altschul, Dr., F.R.G.S., F.R.S.L., F.R.HIST. SOC., &c., Professor of Literature and Elocution
9 Todd & Fletcher, Tailors
10 Holland & Sherry, Woollen Warehousemen
11 Paulig & Co., Furriers
12 Cook, Charles, Furrier
13 Benson & Hedges, Importers of Cigars
Robertshaw, Miss Ann, Governess Agency
13 & 14 Truefitt, H. P., Limited, Hairdressers
Smyth & Nephew, Perfumers
14 Gattie & Peirce, Perfumers
15 Longden Bros., Woollen Warehousemen; and 10 Rue Vivienne, Paris
Lyle, James & Co., Tea Dealers
16 Radley, Edward (late Annoot & Co.), Upholsterer, Cabinet Maker, &c.
17 to 20 Russell & Allen, Silk Mercers
CHURCHILL CHAMBERS:
Adams, F. C.
Avory, H. K.
Low, Capt. George Peter
Gilmour, H. Scott
20 & 21 Robinson & Fisher, Auctioneers

20 Clark, Alfred, Silversmith
21 Miles, Samuel, Military Tailor, &c.
22 Lapworth Bros., Carpet Manufacturers
24 Atkinson, J. & E., Wholesale and Export, Perfumery and Fancy Soap Manufacturers
24 Norton, John, Architect
Masey, Philip Edward, Architect
Here are Burlington Gardens and New Bond Street
25 Benson, Jas. Wm., Watch and Clock Maker
Bassano, Alex., Photographic Artist
Amateur Photographic Association
A. J. Melhuish, F.R.A.S., Hon. Sec.
26 Hays, Alfred, Theatrical Agent
Cock, Jas. Lamborn, Music Publisher
Musical Exchange Limited
Alfred Moul, Secretary
27 Price, N., & Co., Wholesale Perfumers
Westley, Frederick, Optician
BURLINGTON GALLERY
Nathan, Joseph, Dealer in Works of Art
Wallace, William, Architect
Flockhart, William, Architect
Turrell, Charles James, Miniature Painter
Here is the Royal Arcade
29 Haldane, James, Tailor
30 Chapman & Moore, Hatters
31 Binnie & Craggs, Tailors
32 Blue Posts, Charles Wheeler
33 Mitchell, John, Bookseller, &c.
Here is Stafford Street
34 City Bank Ltd., The (Branch Office), Edward G. Mullins, Manager
35 & 36 Bontor, Thomas & Co., Carpet Manufacturers
37 Smith, George W., Jeweller

38 Ollivier, Robert W., Theatrical Ticket Agent
38 Rushbury & Mann, Court Dress Makers
   Harrow & Son, Trunk Makers
39 Bowring, Arundel & Co., Shirt Manufacturers
39b Salomons & Wornum, Architects
   Ball, Wilfrid Williams, Artist
   Agnew, Thomas & Sons, Dealers in Works of Art
   Agnew, William
   Pierre, Dr., Perfumer
40 Steward, Mrs. Elizabeth B., Dairy

Blanc, C. A., & Co., Merchants
Bond, Ernest, & Co., Insurance Agents
41 Oriental Cabinet
42 Armstrong, Geo. & Sons, Grocers
43 Moore, Wm., & Grey, Ltd., Gun Manufacturers
   Highland Sportsman Shooting Agency
   Hall, Robert
44 Whitfield & Sons, Cheesemongers
45 Grunebaum, Joseph, Cigar Merchant
46 Stewart, Francis & Co., Bakers
   Here is Piccadilly

NEW BOND STREET

1 Truefitt, Walter, Hairdresser
2 Piesse & Lubin, Wholesale and Retail Perfumers
   Piesse, Charles H., Public Analyst
3 Dixey, Chas. W., & Son, Opticians
4 Ludlow & Cockburn, Lacemen
   Wilson, Miss A. J., Dressmaker
5 Home & Elliott, Woollen Merchants
   Tulloh, Major Robert Henry
   Johnson, Lieut.-General George Vanderheyden
   Peyton, John Reynolds
6 Taylor & Gardiner, Tailors
7 Gordon & Co., Shirt Makers
8 Thompson & Co., Importers of Cigars
   Levitt, Isaac Lewis
   Morris, Reginald, Barrister
9 Nowlan, John, Bootmaker
   Kerr, William Henry, Chemist and Druggist
10 Pastorelli, Frank & Co., Opticians
10a Midland Railway Co.'s Receiving Office
11 Hillhouse & Co., Hat and Cap Makers
   Toovey, Henry Edmund, Solicitor
12 Muhlenkamp Bros., Shirt Makers
13 & 14 Brown, Wm. Charles, Riding and Fancy Hatter, Furrier, Dressmaker and Costumier
   Brown, Mrs. Wm. Charles, Milliner
16 Long's Family Hotel,
     H. J. Herbert, manager
   Martyn, Rev. Charles, M.A.
   Cooke, Sir Wm. Ridley Charles, Bart.

Lobb, Arthur F.
   Here is Clifford Street
17 London & Ryder (Successors to Hancock), Jewellers, Diamond Merchants, Goldsmiths, Silversmiths, &c.
18 Streeter & Co. (Arthur Pitson), Diamond Merchants, Goldsmiths, Jewellers, Silversmiths and Watchmakers
19 & 20 Redmayne & Co., Silk Mercers
21 Douglas, Robert, Hairdresser
22 Morris, Philip & Co., Cigar Importers
   Speyer, Louis
23 Douglas, Robert, Milliner
23a Callaghan, Wm., & Co., Opticians
   Here is Conduit Street
24 Cadbury, Pratt & Co., Cheesemongers
25 Cadbury, Pratt & Co., Poulterers
   Thomson & Profaze, Watchmakers, removed to 5 Maddox Street, Regent Street W
26 Tessier, Edward, Goldsmith
   Vander & Hedges, Silversmiths
27 Cremer, Wm. Henry, Junior Toy Warehouse
28 Parnacott, Charles, Jeweller
   Parain, Madame Elise, Milliner
29 Ellis & Scrutten, Booksellers
   Cremer, George, & Co., Bootmakers
30 Newson, George, Coach Maker
31 Lucas, Arthur, Print Publisher
   Genty, Madame Eugenie, Corset Maker
   Mathilde, Mademoiselle A., Court Dressmaker

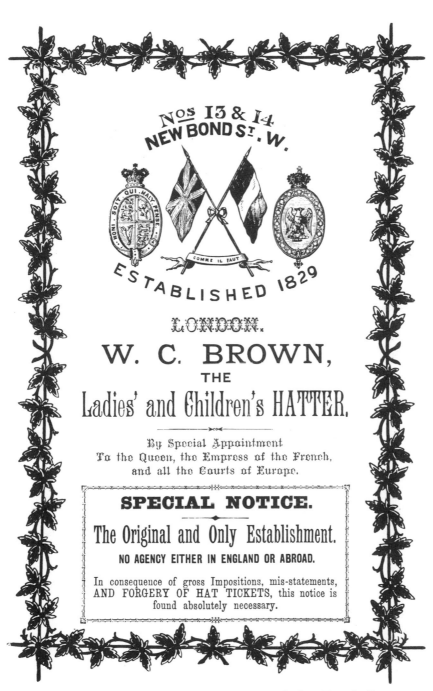

The superbly assured advertisement of the Bond Street
hatters W. C. Brown, published in 1881

32 Harding, Charles Thomas, Florist
33 Davis, Jose, Jeweller
   Palmer, Edward, Waterproof Bootmaker
34 & 35 Woodd, Basil, & Sons, Wine Merchants
34 Clutton, Robert George
35 Doré Gallery,
   Fairless & Beeforth, Proprietors
36 Haseldine, Benjamin, Goldsmith
37 Brockell, William, Shirt Maker
38 Carles Brothers, Peruke Makers
39 Adam, George, & Co., Fruiterers
40 South & Son, Veterinary Surgeons, M.R.C.V.S.
   South, George
41 South, William Alfred
   Williams & Co., Trunk Makers
   Henry, A., Guche & Co., Carriers
42 Hopwood & Crew, Music Publishers
   Coote & Tinney, Quadrille Band
   Knight, Mrs. A., Court Dressmaker
   Hancock, Miss E., Court Milliner
43 Danby Bros., Fancy Fringe Makers
   Berlin Photographic Company,
     August Frederick Schwenckert, sole agent for the United Kingdom
44 Stockley, E., Stationer, &c.
   Boyle's Court Guide Office
45 Burnett & Parrott, Ladies' Outfitters
46 Wells, John Charles, Tailor
   Salmon, Miss Eleanor, Dressmaker
      Here is Maddox Street
47 Hanover Gallery
47a Hargreave, J., & Co., Cigar Merchants
47b Barnett, John W., Printseller
48 Spratt, William Henry, Truss Maker
49, 50, 51 & 52 Chappell & Co., Pianoforte Manufacturers
51 Quarmane, Mrs. Susannah, Private Hotel
52 Chappell, Samuel A., Musical Instrument Maker
   Smith, Richard, Music Publisher
   Vert, Narciso, Musical Agent
   Champion Brass & Military Band Journal
53 Society of Artists,
   Mrs. Atherton, Manageress
   Froebel Society,
     Miss Kate Thornbury, Secretary
   Ball, James Francis, Commission Agent
54 Rimell & Allsop, Tailors

55 Scott, Son & Claxton, Tailors
56 Dollar, Thomas Aitkin, Veterinary Surgeon
57 Leroy & Fils, Watchmakers
   Gabriel, Solomon, Dentist
   Alexander, William, Chiropodist
   Smyth & Nephew, Perfumers, &c
58 & 59 Turner, John, & Co., Goldsmiths
59 Lepri, D., & Co., Fine Art Publishers
60 Shingleton, William, Tailor
   Tupman, Miss Ellen, Dressmaker
61 Holmes, Madame Oliver, Court Dressmaker
62 London Association of Nurses
   Home Hospitals for the Well-to-do (office of)
63 Cramer, J. B., & Co., Theatrical Agents
      Here is Brook Street
64 MacKenna & Dark, Tailors
   Hayward, Madame, Corset Maker
65 Lovell, Miss Maria Eliza, Dressmaker
66 & 65 Hook, Knowles, & Co., Boot Makers
66 Cooper, Mrs. Paxton, Dressmaker
67 Johnstone, Norman, & Co., Cabinet Makers, Upholsterers and House and Estate Agents
   Graham Forster, Cabinet Maker
68 Moret, de la Malmaison, Madame, Court Dressmaker
   Moret, Gabriel, French Polisher
   Ichenhäuser, Julius, Dealer in Works of Art
69 Atloff & Norman, French Bootmakers
   Huggins, Miss Witherington, Court Dressmaker
   Greene, Friese, Photographer
70 Russ, Charles, Manufacturing Furrier
71 Wardle & Co., Oriental Warehouse
72 Perry & Co., Chandelier and Lustre Manufacturers
73 Phillips, Son & Neale, Auctioneers
74 Keene, Ashwell, Headland & Co., Homœopathic Chemists
75 Lockwood, Wm., & Co., Stationers
   Bannister, George
      Here is Union Street
76 Roberts & Co., Foreign Chemists
   Saunders, Thomas S.
78 Masters, Joseph, & Co., Publishers
   Gough, Miss Sarah Ann, Dressmaker

79 Hart, Samuel, Carriage Builder
80 Arrowsmith, Arthur J., & Co., Decorators
81 Blunt & Son, Italian Warehouse
82 Judd, Robert Thomas, Cheesemonger
   Verdon, Mrs. Sarah, Ladies' Outfitter
   Marquis, Mrs. Alice, Governess Agency
83 Grimes, Thomas R., & Son, China Warehouse
84 Lucas (Stanley), Weber, & Co., Music Warehouse
85 Fentum, Martin, Ivory Carver
86 Corbyn, Stacey & Co., Chemists and Druggists
   Hartridge, James Hills
      Here is Oxford Street
87 Harman, John Shipton, Hatter
88 Pillischer, Moritz, Optician, &c.
89 Walpole Bros., Linen Warehouse
   Thrupp, Raymond Henry, Solicitor
   Rodrigues, Jose C.
90 Ellis, Gustav, Furrier
91 Morant & Co., Interior Decorators
   Adolphine, Madame, Dressmaker
92 Williams & Bach, Lamp Manufacturers
93 Kennedy & Smith, Tailors
   Blenheim Restaurant, Mrs. E. Chapman
      Here is Blenheim Street
95 Hopkinson, J. & J., Pianoforte Manufacturers
   Hopkinson, John, F.L.S., F.G.S.
96 Sparrow Bros., Manufacturing Goldsmiths
   Sicklemore, Misses F. & F., Milliners
97 Musgrave & Co. Ltd., Ironfounders
   Salmon, Miss Mary, Dressmaker
   Gorman & Co., Wine Merchants
   Halliday, Thos. Smith, Wine Merchant
98 Holland & Holland, Wholesale Gunmakers
99 Shubrook, Frederic Francis, Tailor
   Valleton, Madame A. M., Dressmaker
100 Coppock, Charles, F.R.A.S., Optician
    Elphick, Madame, Court Dressmaker
    Clarke, Albert John, Stationer
101 Green Man, Mrs. Isabel Stevens
102 Gullick, Thomas John, Art Gallery
    Tapscott, Miss Matilda, Dressmaker
104 Wright & Mansfield, Cabinet Makers
    Collmann, Leonard, Decorator
105 Boyd, Alex., & Son, Ironmongers

Marshall, Miss Isabella Ellen, Dressmaker
106 Donaldson, Geo., Importer of Works of Art
107 Johnson, Joseph, Soap and Candle Maker
108 Lion Booking Office, London & North Western Railway
    Wright, C., & Co., Surgical Instrument Makers
    Donkin, Mrs. Dorothy, Dressmaker
109 Sleight, Misses Elizabeth and Emma, Juvenile Warehouse
    Tuczek, Nikolaus, Bootmaker
110 Lidstone & Co., Butchers
      Here is Brook Street
111 Lawrence & Co., Dealers in Works of Art
    Metcalfe, Miss Helen, Court Dressmaker
112 Ross & Co., Opticians (late 164)
    Walker, Hugh Mewburn
113 Phillips, Solomon J., Silversmith
114 Dickinsons, Portrait Painters
115 Hicks, Wm. Lightit, Dressmaker
116 Perry & Durrant, Ladies' Outfitters
116 & 117 Bousson, Valadon, & Co., Dealers in Works of Art
118 Truckle, George, Photographer
119 Atmospheric Churn Company
    Yeatman & Co., Yeast Powder Manufacturers
    Woolf, Albert M., Glass Paper Agent
120 Ipsen (The) Terra Cotta & Fine Art Pottery
    Arup Bros., Art Pottery Importers
121 Gilson, Wm., & Son, Fishmongers
122 Lord Arran's Arms, William Joseph Gray
      Here is Lancashire Court
123 Lesser, Lesser, Picture Dealer
    Devey, George, Architect
124 Manning, Edward T., & Co., Military Tailors
    McKechnie, Misses Elizabeth and Jean, Court Dressmakers
125 Hardy, John, & Son, Woollen Merchants
126 Huntsman, Henry, Tailor
127 André & Co., Hatters
    French, John, Lodging House
128 Fletcher & Co., Army Tailors
    Eskell & Webb, Dentists
    Lumley, Albert
129 Daniell, R. P., & Co., China Manufacturers

177 Crown (The), Perfumery Co.
   Reeve, Charles Arthur
178 Richards (Westley) & Co., Ltd., Gun-
      makers,
      J. G. Baldwin, Manager
   Hearn, Mrs.
179 Buck & Reid, Fine Art Dealers

   Tofield, Madame, Milliner
180 Dinneford & Co., Chemists
   Grain, R. Corney
   Cooke, Chas. Hy., F.S.A., Architect
   Nevill, Ralph, Architect
      Here is Old Bond Street

In 1911

From *Post Office London Street Directory*, 1911

OLD BOND STREET

1a Scotts, Ltd., Gentlemen's Hatters
1a Scotts, Ltd., Ladies' Hatters
1a Tipton, Thomas B.
1a Meyrowitz, E. B., Optician
2 Royal Copenhagen Porcelain Manufacturing Co.
3 & 4 Hill Brothers, Military Tailors
5 Sandorides, W., & Co., Ltd., Cigarette
   Manufacturers
5 Paterson, Wm. Bell, Fine Art Dealer
5 Gibson (J. S.), Skipwith & Gordon,
   Architects
6 Hummel, E. &. H., & Co., Hosiers
6 Romaine-Walker & Jenkins, Architects
7 Tecla Co., Jewellers
10 & 10a Morgan & Co., Ltd., Coach Builders
11 Haywards', Lacemen
12 Vicars Brothers, Picture Dealers
13 Benson & Hedges, Ltd., Importers of
   Cigars
15a Knoedler, M., & Co., Dealers in Works
   of Art
15 Lyle, Jas., & Co., Ltd., Tea and Coffee
   Dealers
16 Truefitt, H. P., Ltd., Hairdressers
17, 18 & 19 Russell & Allen, Court Dressmakers
20 Klackner, Christian, Fine Art Publisher
21 Duveen Brothers, Experts in Works of
   Art
22 Crichton Brothers, Silversmiths
23a Langfier, Limited, Photographic Artists
23a Berkeley, Mrs. Lilian, Electrolysis
23a Snepp, Alfred Neville
23 Hill, Edwin S., & Co., Hairdressers
24 Atkinson, J. & E., Ltd., Perfumers

24 Wells' Club
25 Benson, J. W., Ltd., Watch Makers
25 Fine Art & General Insurance Co., Ltd.
25 Bassano, Ltd., Photographic Artists
25 Harris, Jonathan, & Sons, Ltd., Linen
   Manufacturers
26 Hays, Alfred, Theatrical Agent
27 Dale, J. R., & Co., Ltd., Ladies' Tailors
27a Wallace, William, Architect
29 Watson Bros., Gun Makers
29 Pomeroy, Mrs., Ltd., Toilet Manufacturers
30 Dreyfous, E., Dealer in Works of Art
31 Charbonnel et Walker, Confectioners
32 Ross, J. & G., Tailors
33 Ashton & Mitchell, Ltd., Theatre Ticket
   Agents
33 Loûfte, Ernest Maximilien, Furrier
34 Dodson Motors, Ltd.
35 Leslie, R., Bill Broker
35 Hanover Dress Co.
35 Orea Cigarette Co.
35 Olyve, Madame M., Skin Specialist
35 Wiberg, John Engelbert, Chiropodist
36 London City and Midland Bank Ltd.
37 Salberg, L. & G., & Co., Glass Makers
37 Morgan, Miss Amy, Manicure
39 Bowring, Arundel & Co., Shirt Makers
40 Antoinette, Madame Marie, French
   Milliner
40 Dey, Thomas Henry, Turf Accountant
41 Pogosky, Madame Alexandra Loginovna,
   Russian Peasant Industries
42 Watherston, James Henry, Jeweller
42 American Tooth Crown Co.
42 Hossack, John Gutzmer, Solicitor

42 Graves, Algernon, Art Expert
43 Agnew, Thomas, & Sons, Dealers in Works of Art
44 Glyn & Co., Manufacturing Hatters
44 Laurens, Ed., Cigarette Manufacturer
45 Heronimos, Apik, Cigarette Manufacturer
46 Armstrong & Sons, Grocers
46 Cullum & Co. (London), Ltd., Cheesemongers
46 Gordon (Ashley) & Co., Land Agents
46 Philippe, Peronne, Hairdresser
47 Connell, Jas., & Sons, Print Sellers
48 Million-Guiet, Motor Body Builders
49 Brown (Kenneth), Baker, Baker & Co., Solicitors

49 Collings, Frank, Picture Gallery
49 D'Artuel et Cie., Complexion Specialists
49 Wright's Patent Teapot Co.
49 Freeman, Sandford, Electric Light Fittings Manufacturer
49 Foulsham & Banfield, Ltd., Photographers
49 Bowen, H., Financier
49 Touboul, E. W., Electric Theatre Proprietor
49 Callard, Stewart & Watt, Ltd.
49 Mollvo, Ivan & Co., Cigarette Manufacturers
49 Arlette, Madame E., Milliner
50 Stewart & Co., Bakers

NEW BOND STREET

1 Truefitt, Walter, Hairdresser
2 Lacloche, Frères, Jewellers
3 Dixey, C. W., & Son, Opticians
4 Grands Magasins Du Louvre
5 Barker, Albert, Ltd., Silversmiths
6 & 7 "Harborows", Glovers
7 Moss, Martin Luther
8 Teresa et Cie, Jewellers
8 Russen, Miss Alice, Milliner
9 Mancus, Harry, Dressmaker
9 Abdulla & Co., Ltd., Cigarette Specialists
10a Midland Railway Co.'s Receiving Office
10 Beth, Madame F. S., Complexion Specialist
10 Gianaclis, Nestor, Cigaratte Manufacturer
10 Nitch-Smith, Reginald, Physician and Surgeon
11 Hillhouse & Co., Hat and Cap Makers
11 Wellbeloved & Newman, Court Dressmakers
12 Muhlenkamp Bros., Shirt Makers
13 & 14 Duchess of Sutherland's Cripples' Guild, Ltd.
13 & 14 Delys, Ltd., Jewellers
13 & 14 Jackson, Miss Beatrice, Electrolysis
13 & 14 Favier, Madame Mary, Dressmaker
14 Weinberg, M., & Co., Cigarette Manufacturers
15a Perà Cigarette Co.
15b Francis, Norman, Ltd., Ladies' Tailors
15 Long's Hotel (Family)
16 Innovation Agency, Trunk Makers

17 London & Ryder, Jewellers
18 Finnigans, Ltd., Makers of Dressing Bags
19 & 20 Redmayne & Co., Ltd., Silk Mercers
21 & 23 Douglas, Robert, Hairdresser
22 Morris, Philip, & Co., Ltd., Cigar Merchants
23 Douglas, Robert, Coiffeur and Posticheur
23a Callaghan, Wm., & Co., Opticians
24 Cadbury, Pratt & Co., Cheesemongers
25 Cadbury, Pratt & Co., Poulterers
26 Vander & Hedges, Goldsmiths
26 Tessier, Edward, Goldsmith
27 Weston, Lambert & Son, Ltd., Photographers
27 Katrina, Madame E., Manicurist
28 London Corset Co.
29 Ellis, Bookseller
29 Duncan & Co., Ladies' Tailors
30 Social Bureau (The), Ltd.
30 Parisian Hat Co., Ltd., Milliners
30 Mattype Co., Photographers
30 Holloway, Miss Florence, Medical Galvanist
31 Fine Art Military and Sporting Gallery, Ltd.
31 Renée, Madame L., Court Dressmaker
32 Marcus, Joseph, Ladies' Tailor
33 Clark, Alfred, Silversmith, &c.
33 Elsie, Mlle. A., Court Milliner
33 Sophie, Madame J., Corsetière
34 & 35 Woodd, Basil, & Sons, Wine and Spirit Merchants

35 Dee, Miss Maud E., Dressmaker
35 Veronique, Ltd., Complexion Specialists
35 Doré Gallery
35 Fishburn, Joseph, Fine Art Dealer
35 Sacred Art Society, Ltd., Fine Art Publishers
35 Acme Investment Co., Ltd.
36 Arthur & Co., Silversmiths
36 Henry, Madame M., Court Dressmaker
37 Stephane, Martial Finette, Blouse Maker
37 Spirella Company of Great Britain, Ltd., Corset Makers
38 Johnson, Herbert, Hat Manufacturer
38 Glazier, Edward John
40 Mellett & Son, Antique Dealers
41 Arthur & Co., Ladies' Tailors
41 Mendelssohn, Ltd., Photographers
41 Bevan, J., Rich Furs, Mantles
42 Adam, G., & Co., F.R.H.S., Florists and Fruiterers
43 & 44 Phillips's, Ltd., China and Glass Merchants
43 & 44 London Electric Treatment Institute, Ltd.
45 & 46 Shamrock Tea Rooms, Ltd.
45 & 46 Cross, Alfred William Stephens, M.A., Architect
45 & 46 Anstey, Mrs. Henry, Shopping Adviser
45 & 46 Barréiros, Madame Berthe, Corsetière
45 & 46 Williams, Miss Evelyn, Complexion Specialist
46 Williams, W., & Co., Ltd., Trunk Makers
47 & 48 Pinet, F., Boot and Shoe Maker
47 & 48 Seymour, Madame Handley-, Dressmaker
50 Chappell & Co., Ltd., Music Publishers
51 White House Linen Specialists, Ltd.
51 Fanoni & Morighetti, Private Family Hotel
52 Society of Artists
52 Paris Dress Stand Co.
52 Phillips, Reginald M., Estate Agent
52 Heinz, Hugo, Teacher of Singing
52 Albion Concert Bureau
53 White, Carlton, Florist
54 Rimell and Allsop, Tailors
55 Humphrey, E., Ltd., Furriers

56 Dollar, Thomas Aitken, & Sons, Veterinary Surgeons
57 Le Roy & Fils, Watch Makers
58 & 60 Taylor, Madame Maude, Ladies' Outfitter
58 Hart (Harry S.), Bayne & Co., Variety Agents
59 Gray, A., & Co., Constructional Engineers
59 Weihs, Morris, Furrier
60 & 58 Taylor, Madame Maude, Ladies' Outfitter
60 Kosmeo, Arthur, Toilet Requisites
60 Bayne, Harry & Co., Underclothing Agents
61 Bond, Chas., & Son, Wig Makers
61 Modern Gallery (The)
61 Freeman, Edward, Fine Art Commission Agent
61 Baudet, A., & Co., Manufacturers' Agents
61 Austen, Anne, Ltd., Dealers in Antiquities
62 Louvet Frères (Grand Maison de Blanc), Linen Drapers
62 & 63 Fenwick, Ltd., Ladies' Tailors
63 Gunter & Co., Ltd., Confectioners
65 Lovell, Miss M. E., Court Dressmaker
65 & 66 Hook, Knowles & Co., Ltd., Boot Makers
67 & 68 Hayward, Madame A. M., Court Dressmaker
67 & 68 Cassels, Miss Amy, Photographer
69 Montague, John Henry, Surgical Instrument Maker
69 Trost, Madame Bertha, Complexion Specialist
69 Widgery, Madame Tucker, Milliner
69 Hernestus, C., Ladies' Tailor
70 Russ & Co., Furriers
70 Kinrade, Miss Fanny, Court Dressmaker
71 Rhee, Ellison & Co., Tailors
71 Gauterie Parisienne Co., Glovers
71 Alexander, William, Chiropodist
72 Keele, J., Ltd., Motor Car Agents
72 Debenham, Austen & Co., House Agents
72 Wright, James Thomas, Tailor
72 Watson, Mrs. Delia, Manicure
72 Sommer, Emil, Ladies' Tailor
73 Phillips, Son & Neale, Auctioneers
74 Wase, Charles, Confidential Agent

147

74 Clements, Miss Kate, Manicure
75 Lockwood, Wm., & Co., Stationers
75 Fisher, Samuel, Ladies' Tailor
76 Roberts & Co., Foreign and English Chemists
77 Pickett, William James, Tailor
77 Streur, Maurice Frederick, Perfumery Agent
77 Lotty, Madame C., Corsetière
78 Bond Street Fur Co.
79 Barbellion, Leopold, Confectioner
80
81 Shanks & Co., Ltd., Ironfounders
81 Hussey, Ltd., Gun Makers
82 & 83 Benson, W. A. S., & Co., Ltd., Metal Workers, &c.
82 & 83 London Glove Co.
84 Wayre, Charles & Co., Furriers
85 Parisian Diamond Co., Ltd.
85 Neroma Syndicate Ltd.
86 Hitching's, Ltd., Perambulator Manufacturers
87 Harman & Son, Hatters
88 Pillischer, Jacob, Optician
88 May, Carl, Ladies' Tailor
89 & 90 Walpole Bros., Ltd., Linen Manufacturers
90 Haseldine, Percy, Goldsmith
90 Douglas, Wm. Core, Interior Decorator
91 Morant & Co., Interior Decorators
91 Johnstone, Norman, & Co., Cabinet Makers
91 Gregg, James Shirley, Glover
91 Courtoise, Mesdames Hélène and Renée, Photographers
92 Cooling, John Albert, Picture Dealer
92 Adair, Mrs. Eleanor, Complexion Specialist
93 Bill, W., Homespun Merchant
94 & 124 Lyons, J., & Co., Ltd., Café
95 Lanchester Motor Co., Ltd. (The)
95 London Fashions Publishing Co., Ltd.
95 Hagelmann, Wm., & Son, Tailors
96 Smith, William Bryan, Tailor
96 Cattle, Miss Helen, Court Dressmaker
97 Sampson & Co., Shirt Makers
97 Lines, J. Calvin, Hosier
97 McKenna & Co., Solicitors
97 McEwan, Oliver, Teacher of Shorthand
97 Walder-Wallis, Mrs. Constance, Teacher of Singing
98 Holland & Holland, Ltd., Gun Makers
99 Deimel (Dr.), Underwear Co.
100 Bramah & Co (Needs & Co.), Patent Lock Makers
100 Elphick, Madame Frances, Court Dressmaker
102 Lang, Joseph, & Son, Ltd., Gun Makers
102 Paterson, John, Court Hairdresser
102 Hélène, Madame H., Corset Maker
103 Ramsden, Archibald, Ltd., Pianoforte Importers
104 Larkin, Thomas Joseph, Dealer in Antiquities
105 Coulson, Wm., & Sons, Linen Manufacturers
105 & 106 Standard Range & Foundry Co., Ltd.
105 & 106 Allan & Co., Court Dressmakers
105 & 106 Smith, Jas., & Sons, Ltd., Builders
105 & 106 Brooke, Miss Belinda, Electrolysis
105 & 106 Betts, Mrs. Arthur J., Ladies' Hatter
105 & 106 Leighton & Joseph, Blouse Manufacturers
105 & 106 Theosophical Society in England and Wales
106 Adams Manufacturing Co., Ltd., Electrical Engineers
106 Swaine, Frank Arthur, Photographer
107 London Soap & Candle Co.
107 Charles, Madame Marie, Court Dressmaker
108 St. George's Gallery
108 de Roy, Madame Claire, Dressmaker
108 London & North-Western Railway Booking Office
109 Sleight, Misses E. & E., Milliners
109 Cucchiara, Angelo, Teacher of Languages
110 Friswell (1906), Ltd., Automobile Engineers
111 Ross, Limited, Opticians
112 & 114 Irish Linen Stores (The)
113 Phillips, Solomon J., Silversmith
113 Rose, John, Chiropodist
113 Darby, Madame Frances, Court Dressmaker

170 Millinery Manufacturing Co., Ltd.
171 Foot, J., & Son, Ltd., Invalid Furniture Manufacturers
171 Wales, H. A., Co. (The), Acoustic Instrument Makers
171 Collings, Esmé, Photographer
172 Sabin, Frank Thomas, Bookseller
172 Johnson, Walker & Tolhurst, Ltd., Diamond Merchants
172 Quest Gallery (The)
173 Fabergé, C., Jewellers
174 Evans & Mason, Tailors
174 Ladies' Own Hat Co., Ltd., Milliners
174 Normand, Mrs. Anna, Business Training School

174 Seymour, W. A. & Co., Cigarette Manufacturers
175 Williamson, Delmar, Teacher of Singing
175 & 176 Cartier, A., & Son, Jewellers
177 Harman & Co., Ltd., Diamond Merchants
178 Richards (Westley) & Co., Ltd., Gun Makers
178 Middlesex Gun Club
178 & 179 Lafayette, Ltd., Photographers
178 Jules Mignard, Ladies' Hairdresser
179 Pitson, Arthur, Goldsmith
180 Partridge, Lewis & Simmons, Dealers in Works of Art

In 1938

From *Post Office London Street Directory*, 1938

OLD BOND STREET

1 Scotts Limited, Gents' Hatters
1a Scotts Limited, Ladies' Hatters
1a Tipton, Harold T.
1a Meyrowitz, E. B., Ltd., Opticians
2 Lacon & Ollier, Theatre Ticket Office

2 to 5 STANBROOK HOUSE:
FIRST FLOOR
Red Line Power & Heat Services
Kitchen Planning Centre, Kitchen Planning Contractors
SECOND FLOOR
Gould, Barbara, Ltd., Complexion Specialists
Parfums Chanel Ltd., Wholesale Perfumers
Bourjois Ltd., Manufacturing Perfumers
Biondi, Marie, Dressmaker
THIRD FLOOR
Frobisher Trust Ltd.
Roditi Bros., Ltd., General Merchants
Amalgamated Property Society Ltd., Property Owners
Rolfe de Paris Ltd., Manufacturing Perfumers
Hand & Nail Culture Institute Ltd.
Marcus, Mrs. Rose, Dressmaker
FOURTH FLOOR
Anglo-Continental Wine & Spirit Co., Ltd.

Brown Percy's School of Fashion
Williams Enterprises Ltd., Business Agents
Caribonum Ltd., Typewriter Ribbon and Carbon Manufacturers
FIFTH FLOOR
Spencer Corsets Ltd.
Wendy Fashions Ltd., Surgical Belt Makers
Howard & Wyndham Ltd., Theatre Proprietors

3 MacConnal, Rayner, Fine Art Dealer
4 Commercial Bank of Scotland, Ltd.
5 Thorp, Thos., Bookseller
6 Royal Copenhagen Porcelain Co., Ltd.

6, 7 & 8 OLD BOND STREET HOUSE:
GROUND FLOOR
Embassy Club Ltd.
FIRST FLOOR
Standard Products Co., Sectional Bookcase Manufacturers
Bell, Alfred, & Co., Ltd., Fine Art Publishers
British Cine-Alliance Ltd., Film Production
SECOND FLOOR
Romaine-Walker, & Jenkins, Architects
Simmonds, Hunter, Turf Commission Agent

Théiron School of Life, Ltd.
  THIRD FLOOR
Parkfield Trust (1935) Ltd.
Elizabeth, Manicurist
Sagar, Arthur, Financial Broker
Bristow, T. F., & Co., Ltd., Toilet Soap
  Makers
  FOURTH FLOOR
Pilditch, Chadwick & Co., Architects
River Taxis Ltd.
Neame, Elwin, Photographic Artist

7 Tecla (London) Gem Co., Ltd., Jewellers
9 Barrett, W., & Son, Ltd., Brush Makers
10 & 10a Armstrong Siddeley Motors Ltd.
11 Hellstern & Sons Ltd., Boot Makers
11 Bramahs Ltd., Lock Makers
11 Haymarket & City Window Cleaning Co.
11 Cameron, Colin, & Co., Turf Accountants
12 Vicars Brothers Ltd., Picture Dealers
13 Benson & Hedges Ltd., Cigar Merchants
13 Teofani & Co., Ltd., Cigarette Manu-
    facturers
13 Ledger, J., & Son, Fine Art Dealers
14 Pope & Bradley, Tailors
15 Knoedler, M., & Co., Inc., Dealers in
    Works of Art
16 Delman Ltd., Hand-made Shoes
16 Soignée Ltd., Health & Beauty Service
16 Factor, Max, Hollywood & London (Sales)
    Ltd., Cosmetics
16 Music Corporation of America Ltd.,
    Theatrical Agents
16 Hammond, Bertha M., Ltd., Hair Treatment
17 & 18 Canby, Ladies' Handbag Makers
17 & 18 Del End, Ladies' Shoes
19 Dixey, C. W., & Son, Ltd., Opticians
20 Bag Shop Ltd., Ladies' Fancy Bags
21 Gieves Ltd., Tailors
22 Crichton Bros., Silversmiths
22 Pearce, Leighton, Sculptor
22 Wilding, Miss Dorothy, Photographer
22 Arlington Galleries Ltd.
22 Royal Society of Miniature Painters,
    Sculptors & Gravers
23 Truefitt, Hill Ltd., Hairdressers
24 Atkinson, J. & E., Ltd., Perfumery Manu-
    facturers
24 Kell, Josephine, Ltd., Beauty Specialists
24 Jacks, Marian, Ltd., Corsetières

24 Paris Academy of Dressmaking Ltd.
Here are Burlington Gardens and New Bond Street
25 Benson, J. W., Limited, Watch and Clock
    Makers
25 Hunt & Roskell Ltd., Jewellers
25 Arden, Elizabeth, Skin Specialist
26 Hays, Alfred, Ltd., Music Publishers
26 Bognor Estates Ltd.
27 Sulka, A., & Co., Ltd., Shirt Makers

27 ARCADE HOUSE:
    FIRST FLOOR
Catering Equipment Ltd.
Melachrino, M., & Co., Ltd., Cigarette
  Manufacturers
    SECOND FLOOR
Lyon, Mrs. Lilian L., Milliner
Crescent Preparations Co., Ltd., Manu-
  facturing Chemists
Horcher Ltd., Caterers
Verrando, Angélé, Milliner
Armanda, Milliner
Scott, J. D., & Son, Tailors
Lady Clare, Gowns
Ingham, F. & W., Travel Organizers
    THIRD FLOOR
Laleek, Beauty Preparations
Hallett, W., & Co., Estate Agents
Raie, Gowns
Klytia Ltd., Beauty Preparations
Marrdo, Wholesale Milliners
Parfums Lucien Leloag Ltd., Wholesale
  Perfumers
Prestedge, Percy E., Chiropodist
Broadbridge, Sir George Thomas,
  K.C.V.O., F.R.G.S., F.C.I.S.
    FOURTH FLOOR
More, O'Ferrall, Ltd., Advertising Agents
  and Contractors
Anglo-Irish Insurance & Blood Stock
  Agency Ltd.
Neatby, Margery, Milliner
Brook, G. R. C., & Co., Publishers
Brassey, Miss E. L. Chiropodist
Shepherd, Miss Victoria, Pearl Stringer
Zuric Ltd., Plastic Moulding Manufac-
  turers
Mackenzie, Mrs., Ltd., Electrolysis
    FIFTH FLOOR
Brandon, Henry, Private Estate Office

Gossamer, Lingerie
Paul, Photographer
Truman, Miss Joan, Refreshment Rooms

Here is the Royal Arcade

28 Dolland & Aitchison Ltd., Opticians
29 Holmes (Jewellers) Ltd., Silversmiths
29 Pomeroy, Mrs., Ltd., Electrolysis and Complexion Specialists
30 Fanchon Ltd., Boot and Shoe Makers
30 Thamar, Madame, Ltd., Beauty Specialists
30 Norman, Ladies' Hairdresser
30 Wallace, Miss E., Manicurist
30 Fernande, Madame, & Hunt, Anna, Dressmakers
31 Charbonnel & Walker Ltd., Chocolate Manufacturers
32 Jourado Ltd., Jewellers
33 Yardley & Co., Ltd., Perfumery Makers
33 Corot Ltd., Court Dressmakers

Here is Stafford Street

34 Skinner & Co., Jewellers
35 Orea Cigarette Co.
35 Sandown Park Club
35 Sandown Park Ltd.
35 Maria, Madame, Ladies' Hairdresser
35 Wiberg, Harold Gordon, Chiropodist
35 Howard Young Galleries Ltd., Picture Dealers
35 Carr, Miss Lennox, Employment Agency
35 French Gallery
35 Ey-Teb, Beauty Specialists
36 Midland Bank Ltd.
37 Feódar Ltd., Milliners
38 Charig Ltd., Jewellers
38 Innoxa (England) Ltd., Toilet Preparations

39 Lloyds Bank Ltd.
40 Powell, Albert Edward, Court Glover
40 Rowland, Mary Scott, Ltd., Toilet Requisites
41 Sainsbury, S., Ltd., Chocolate Makers
42 Davis & Sons, Dyers, London, Ltd.
42 Council of Justice to Animals
42 Cruwys, Tailor
42 Gainsborough, Estelle, Ltd., Beauty Salon
42 Barlow & Co., Turf Commission Agents
43 Agnew, Thos., & Sons, Ltd., Dealers in Works of Art
44 Kirkby & Bunn, Jewellers
44 Verdi, Madame Suzanne, Complexion Specialists
45 Heronimos, A., Cigarette Manufacturer
45 Pasquali Cigarette Co., Ltd.
45 Goldschmidt, E. P., & Co., Ltd., Antique Booksellers
47 District Bank Ltd.
48 Ciro Pearls Ltd.
49 Fink, Harry Jay, Cereal Products
49 Scott, John, & Clarence, W., Chiropodists
49 Morgan, Miss Amy, Manicurist
49 Overseas Cars Ltd., Motor Car Agents
49 Lamberts, Parkers & Gaines (Established 1740) Ltd., Wine Shippers
49 Cochran, Charles Blake, Theatrical Manager
49 Conrad & Co., Ltd., Turf Commission Agents
49 Horley & Co., Ltd., Turf Accountants
49 Heathorn, A., Ltd., Turf Commission Agents
50 Stewart & Co., Manufacturing Confectioners

Here is Piccadilly

NEW BOND STREET

1 National Provincial Bank Ltd.
1 to 5 Woolworth, F. W., & Co., Ltd.
1 Lytle, C. J., Ltd., Advertising Consultants
1 Condé, Nast Publications, Ltd., Publishers
2 Coty Parfums de Luxe
3 Lacloche Frères, Jewellers
4 Breves Lalique Galleries
5 Tyme Ltd., Watch Manufacturers
6 & 7 Harborow's Ltd., Glovers, Shirt Makers and Hosiers
8 Eos, Court Dressmaker

9a Joanny Ltd., Ladies' Shoe Makers
9 Lurgans, Ladies' Tailors
10a Tully, B. J., Jeweller
10 Smith (L. C.), & Corona, Typewriters Ltd.
10 Glover, H. & E., General Merchants
10 Smith, Peter, A.R.I.B.A., Architect
10 Pym, John, A.R.I.B.A., Architect
10 Mendelssohn, Heinrich, Progress Building Ltd.
10 Rachlis, Michael, Architect

11 Hillhouse & Co., Hat and Cap Makers
11 Bourne, Ltd., Manufacturing Jewellers
11 Terese & Cree, Manicurists
12 Hummel, E. & H., & Co., Ltd., Hosiers
13 Maxie, Gowns
13 & 14 Hudson, Ivy, Ltd., Milliners
13 & 14 Rosen, B. S., Insurance Broker
13 & 14 Rhodes, B. S., Ltd., Money Lenders
13 & 14 Jackson, Miss Beatrice, Electrolysis
13 & 14 Wetherall, Sports Wear Dealers
14 Sessel, Jeweller
15a Péra Cigarette Co.
15b Jensen, Georg, (Silversmiths), Ltd.
15 Santá Ltd., Ladies' Hatters
16 Boots The Chemists

Here is Clifford Street

17 London & Ryder (Proprietors, Finnigans Ltd.), Goldsmiths and Jewellers
17, 18, 19 & 20 Finnigans Ltd., Actual Makers: Trunks, Dressing Bags, &c.
18 Fischers Restaurant
20 Jevons, Janet, Ltd., Photographers
20 Silvester, Victor, Dancing School
21 & 23 Douglas, Robert (Bond Street), Ltd., Coiffeurs and Posticheurs
22 Morris, Philip, & Co., Ltd., Cigar Merchants
23 Ayala (London) Ltd., Champagne Shippers
23 & 21 Douglas, Robert (Bond Street) Ltd., Sports Wear
23a Callaghan, William, & Co., Ltd., Opticians
23a Henri, H., Ladies' Tailor

Here is Conduit Street

24 Cadbury, Pratt & Co., Ltd., Cheesemongers
24 Rita, Court Dressmaker
24 Curtis, J., Ltd., Financiers
24 Prioleau & Grigg, Milliners
25 Cadbury, Pratt & Co., Ltd., Poulterers
26 Tessiers Ltd., Goldsmiths, Silversmiths and Jewellers
27 Surman (Bond St.) Ltd., Lingerie, Dresses
28 Blairman, H., & Sons, Works of Art Dealers
28 Hörnés, Maria, Ltd., Facial Culture
28 Bouchard Ltd., Hairdressers
29 Somerset, Marjorie, Ltd., Milliners
30 Collison, Mrs. (Outfitters), Ltd., Ladies' Outfitters

31 Uchenka Ltd., Gowns
32 Hart, Albert, & Co., Furriers
33 Barri Ltd., Court Dressmakers
34 & 35 Sotheby & Co., Auctioneers
35 Smith, W. H., & Son, Ltd., Newsagents
36 Arthur & Co., Jewellers
36 Davis, Reginald, Antique Silver Dealer
36 Henry, Madame, Ltd., Court Dressmaker
36 Pearce, Stella Mary, Ltd., Court Dressmakers
36 Jill, Madame, Milliner
36 Smout, P. Libbis, Accountant
37 Lewis & Lewis (Bond St.), Ltd., Fine Art Dealers
37 Linn, John F., Ladies' Tailor
37 Bottin, Madame Elise, corsetière
37 Hume, Miss Kitty, Dressmaker
37 Paterson, James, Hair Specialist
38 Johnson, Herbert (Bond St.), Ltd., Hat Manufacturers
38 Glazier, Edward John
40 Mallett & Son, Antique Dealers
41 Janice Ltd., Gowns
41 Gant, Daniel M., Turf Commission Agent
41 Judy, Sportswear Dealer
41 McGuire, Mrs., Ltd., Electro Therapy
41 Marguerite, Massage
41 Evans, David T., Chiropodist
41 Humphrey's School of Dancing
41 Reece (1932) Ltd., Gowns
41 Wrightson, Hay, Photographer
41 Permanent Complexion Tinting Ltd.
42 Adam, G., & Co., F.R.H.S., Florists and Fruiterers
43 Rodier Ltd., Woollen Manufacturers
43 London Beauty Culture & Hairdressing School Ltd.
44 Tiffany & Co., Jewellers
45 Krosky, Gene, Ltd., Gowns
46 Yunda Beauty Culture Ltd., Complexion Specialists
45 & 46 Barréiros, Madame Berthe, Corsetière
45 & 46 Chantrey, Madame Alys, Ltd., Toilet Requisites
45 & 46 Cross, A. W. S. & K. M. B., Architects
45 Hubbard, George, & Son, Architects
46 Lafarge, George, Ladies' Handbag Maker
46a Watson, Alexander M., Embosser

Here is Maddox Street

47 & 48 Pinet, F., Boot and Shoe Maker
47 & 48 Handley, Seymour, Ltd., Court Dressmakers
50 Chappell & Co. Limited, Music Publishers
50 Chappell Piano Co. Ltd.
51 & 52 White House (Linen Specialists) Ltd.
53 Brandt Ltd., Antique Dealers
53 to 55 Rimell & Allsop Ltd., Tailors
53 to 55 Rimasop Ltd., Woollen Merchants
53 to 55 Barri Ltd., Court Dressmakers (Office)
54 Smythson, Frank, Ltd., Stationers
55 Galloway Reels, Woollen Manufacturers
55 Edinburgh Weavers, Furnishing Fabrics
55 Nox Ltd., Builders
56 Tissus, Grenot, Ltd., Novelty Fabric Manufacturers
57 Le Roy et Fils Ltd., Jewellers
58 Rayne, H. & M., Ltd., Shoe Makers
58 Etta & Twine Ltd., Wholesale Milliners
59 Magg, Court Dressmaker
60 & 63 Fenwick Ltd., Gowns
60 Services Pari-Mutuel Ltd.
60 Travis, Eileen, Dressmaker

Here is Brook Street

64 Royal Bank of Scotland
64 Barry, Margaret, Ltd., Milliners
65 Bentley & Co., Jewellers
65 Wright's Detective Agency
65 Anglo-Continental Guest Bureau, Estate Agents
65 Graymonts, General Merchants
66 Smith, (W. H.), & Hook, Knowles & Co., Ltd., Boot Makers
66 Camilla Ltd., Dressmakers
66 Monno, Madame Jane, Milliner
67 Dawson, A., Ltd., Manufacturing Furriers
68 Jean, Gowns
68 Bonds Restaurant Ltd.
69 Paget, Gowns
69 Weiss, Edward, Ltd., Wholesale Furriers
70 Barbellion, Maison (1933), Ltd., Caterers
70 Stetson Hats
70 Directors Club (The)
70 Moirée Ltd., Gowns
70 Molly, Madam, Milliner
70 Kent, Elizabeth, Ladies' Hairdresser
70 Deborah Ltd., Wholesale Costume Makers

70 Cubitt & Manger, Gown Manufacturers
70 Bushe, G. Scott, Ltd., Commercial Photographers
71 Morley, Claire, Ltd., Gowns
71 Brown, Mrs. Frazer, Electrolysis
72 Gunter & Co., Ltd., Caterers
72 Puttick & Simpson, Auctioneers
72 Burnet, D., Ladies' Hairdresser
72 Adèle & Marek (J.), Ladies' Tailors
73 Cresta Silks Ltd., Silk Mercers
73 Marina, Millinery
73 Academy of Beauty Culture Ltd.
73 Kocher, Arthur, Ladies' Tailor
73 Carbel Watch Co., Ltd., Watch Manufacturers
73 Applied Heat Co., Furnace Builders
73 Hartley, Gertrude M., Beauty Specialist
73 Phillips' Auction Rooms
73 Brygos Gallery, Fine Art Dealers
73 Kay, A. C., Silk Mercers
73 Levy's Sound Studios Ltd.
74 Roussel, Maison J., Corsetières
74 Courier Service Employment Agency
74 Sudbury, Arthur E., Lace Agent
74 London Fashion Staff Bureau
74 London Mannequin School
74 Partoon & Paul Ltd., Tailors
75 Hacking, B. M., Ltd., Gowns

Here is Dering Street

76 Roberts & Co., Foreign and English Chemists
76 Cargueray, Mademoiselle Eglantine, Corsetière
77 Pickett, William James, Tailor
77 Kerka Permanent Waving Ltd., Ladies' Hairdressers
78 Vere, Gowns
78 Vigor Permanent Waving Co.
78 Thomas, W. J., Tailor
79 Jays Linen Co., Ltd.
80 Vienna Sports Ltd., Sportswear Dealers
80 Leslie, Ladies' Hairdressers
80 New Furs for Old Ltd., Retail Furriers
80 Kasher, Marks, Ladies' Tailor
81 Shanks & Co., Ltd., Sanitary Appliance Manufacturers
82 & 83 London Glove Co., Ltd.
84 Singer Sewing Machine Co., Ltd.
84 Clarke & Clarke, Estate Agents
84 Simmons, Lewis, Ladies' Tailor

85 Linden & Co. (New Bond St.), Ltd., Jewellers

85 & 86 Exo Ltd., Leather Goods, Metal Frames

86 Dolcis Shoe Co., Boot Makers

86 Moss, Alfred E., Dentist

86 Roberts, S. Halford, Dentist

86 Redex Proprietaries Ltd., Pharmaceutical Preparations

86 Domestic Electrification Ltd.

Here is Oxford Street

87 to 91 Walpole Bros. (London), Ltd., Linen Manufacturers

87 to 91 Lucas, Otto, Ltd., Wholesale Milliner

87 to 91 Golanski, A., & Co., Manufacturing Furriers

87 Jean, Norman, Ltd., Lingerie Makers

87 to 91 Myer Emporium (London) Ltd., Australian Merchants

87 to 91 Associated Merchandising Corporation, American Merchants

92 Cooling Galleries Ltd., Picture Dealers

93 Bill, W., Ltd., Homespun Specialists; Hosiery and Knitwear

93 Stafford, Mrs. B. A., Wholesale Gown Maker

94 Wetherall, Sportswear Dealers

94 Berkeley Club

94 Lantern Restaurant

Here is Blenheim Street

95 Netta (Gowns) Ltd.

95 Bond Street Bridge Club

96 Moss, Lydia, Ltd., Lingerie Dealers

96 Swerling, Miss Chrissie, Wholesale Milliner

97 Sampson & Co., Shirt Makers (now W. Hayford & Sons), removed to 202 to 205 Sloane Street, SW1

98 Holland & Holland Limited, Gun Makers

99 Deimel Fabric Co., Manufacturers of Dr. Deimel Underwear

99 Brainin Bros., Manufacturing Furriers

99 Alexander, Gladys, Ltd., Hairdressers

99 Rudd, Jane, Ltd., Wholesale Gown Manufacturers

100 Rayner & Keeler Ltd., Opticians

101 Corine, Milliner

101 Savio, A., Ltd., Ladies' Tailors

102 Myers & Co., Booksellers

103 Brooklands Motor Co., Motor Car Dealers

105 Coulson, Wm., & Sons, Linen Manufacturers

105 & 106 Rowe, William, & Co., Ltd., School Outfitters

105 & 106 Beresford & Smith Ltd., Turf Commission Agents

106 Neilson Studio, Photographers

107 Froy, W. N., & Sons, Ltd., Builders' Merchants

107 Croft, Maxwell, Ltd., Wholesale Furriers

107 Perquin, Michael, Ladies' Tailor

108 Gordon, Mrs. Lesmoir, Dog Bureau Ltd.

108 London, Midland & Scottish Railway General Booking & Inquiry Office for Passengers, Parcels and Goods

109 Tallula Ltd., Milliners

110 Reinli-Hayes Ltd., Ladies' Shoe Manufacturers

110a Footprints, Textile Block Printers

Here is Brook Street

112, 113, 114 & 115 Givans Irish Linen Stores Ltd.

113 Philips, S. J., Silversmith

115 Mudie & Sons Ltd., Stationers

116 & 117 London Shoe Co., Ltd.

118 Walker's Galleries Ltd., Fine Art Publishers

118 Ladies' League (The), Employment Agency

118 Nella Ltd., Gowns

118 Entwistle, Clive, Architect

119 Sketchley Dye Works

119 Dummett, B. M., & Co., Tobacconists

119 Arnold, Marie (London) Ltd., Beauty Culture

119 Kyril, Milliners

121 Duvellerory, J., Ltd., Fan Manufacturers

121 Goodwin & Son Ltd., Estate Agents

121 Lethbridge, Gwendoline, Skin Specialist

122 Ariane Ltd., Gowns

Here is Lancashire Court

123 Russer, Miss Alice, Dressmaker

123 Davies, Robert J., Antique Dealer

123 Davies, Eliz., Wholesale Milliner

123 Campbell, John, Turf Commission Agent

123 Fores, Geo. P., Printseller

124 Lyons, J., & Co., Ltd., Café

124 Mlinaric, Matjaz, Furrier

124 New Bond Co., Ltd., Manufacturing Clothiers

124 Collier, Madame Adèle, Teacher of Dancing

160 Duveen, John, Art Expert
160 Morris (E. G.), Mantle, & Co., Ltd., Insurance Brokers
161 Barclays Bank Ltd.
161 Parkington, J. R., & Co., Ltd., Wine Merchants
161 Patent Marketing Co., Ltd., General Merchants
161 Tomlinson, Clarence S., Solicitor
161 Sykes, Chas., Architect
161 Harlip Ltd., Photographers
163 Powder Box Ltd., Complexion Specialists
163 & 164 Hermine Ltd., Gowns
Here is Grafton Street
165 to 169 Asprey & Co., Ltd., Goldsmiths, Silversmiths, Jewellers, Watch and Clock Makers, Dressing Bag and Trunk Makers, Fine Leather Workers, &c.
170 Maison Nicol Ltd., Hairdressers
171 Chalmaux, Milliner
171 Dey, Thomas Henry, Ltd., Turf Accountants
172 Heath, Henry, Ltd., Hat Manufacturers

173 Abdulla & Co., Ltd., Tobacco Manufacturers
174 Daniell, Major, Ltd., Tailors
174 Schwaiger, Imré, Art Expert
174 Cooper, Szabo & d'Ehrmanns, Ltd., Chinese Works of Art
175 & 176 Cartier Ltd., Jewellers
177 Harman & Lambert, Goldsmiths
178 Savory, H. L., & Co., Ltd., Cigar Importers
178 Stenning, Constance, Beauty Specialist
178 Opas, B., Tailor
178 Westley, Richards & Co., Ltd., Gun and Rifle Makers, removed to 23 Conduit Street W.1
179 Goat Club Ltd.
179 Drayson, Cecil, Ltd., Jewellers
180 Boucheron Ltd., Jewellers
180 Dew, John, Ltd., Milk Soap Manufacturers
180 Bartlett, Dixon & Co., Ltd., Tourist Agents
Here is Old Bond Street

In 1978

From *Post Office London Directory*, 1978

OLD BOND STREET

1 Tyme Ltd., Watchmakers
1 Gerrard, Laurence & Co., Chartered Accountants
1a Meyrowitz, E. B., Ltd., Opticians
1a Elkwerth & Co., Ltd., Wholesale Opticians
1a British Lens Co. (Export) Ltd.
2 Goode, Thos., & Co. (London) Ltd., China and Glass Merchants
3 Ackermann, Arthur, & Son, Ltd., Picture Dealers

2 to 5 STANDBROOK HOUSE:
FIRST FLOOR
Hapag-Lloyd (U.K.), Ltd., Shipping Line
Tritube Ltd., Tube Merchants
Euroselect Executive Consultants Ltd.
SECOND FLOOR
Chanel Ltd., Perfumers
Bourjois Ltd., Manufacturing Perfumers

THIRD FLOOR
C.A.M. Saunders Ltd., Management Selection Consultants
Lumley, Thomas, Ltd., Antique Silver
Dolphin Maritime & Aviation Services Ltd., Air Charter Brokers
McCarthy & Bainbridge, Quantity Surveyors
Cuthbertson, W. A., Ltd., Management Consultants
Hayward Travel, Travel Agents
FOURTH FLOOR
Asia Magazines Ltd.
Barriman, Anthony, & Co., Property Consultants
Global Marine Europa Ltd., Offshore Drilling Contractors
FIFTH FLOOR
Itavia Airlines

British American Chamber of Commerce, N.Y.

International Tours Centre

Associated Products (England) Ltd., Toilet Preparations

Bennett, Newbery & Cowan, Marketing Consultants

Frenbury Properties Ltd., Property Developers

Neville, Rodie & Shaw, Investment Consultants

4 Fenzi, Menswear
5 Royal Copenhagen Porcelain Co., Ltd.
6 Hills Cashmere House, Knitwear
8 Mayfair Carpet Gallery, Carpet Retailers

6, 7 & 8 OLD BOND STREET HOUSE:
GROUND FLOOR
Embassy Club
FIRST FLOOR
Crinnan (Jewellery) Ltd., Manufacturing Jewellers
Sado & King Ltd., Wine Merchants
SECOND FLOOR
Duncan Miller & Associates Ltd., Sales Promotion Consultants
THIRD FLOOR
Phonesales Ltd., Sales Promotion Services
Noise Abatement Society
FOURTH FLOOR
Europa Shoes Ltd., Footwear Importers
Sierra Productions Ltd., Film Producers

9 Zubair, D., Ltd., Carpet Retailers
9 Kent, Howard, Consultancy, Public Relations
9 Barker, A., & Sons, Ltd., Boot and Shoe Manufacturers
9 Vossen-Frottier (U.K.) Ltd., Towel Manufacturers
9 Intercapital Travellers Ltd., Travel Agents
9 Yoga for Health Clubs, Physical Culture Institute
10 Argos Distributors Ltd., Discount House
10 Lufthansa German Airlines (Administration)
11 Brainin Cashmeres, Exclusive Knitwear
11 Katz, Wm., Picture Dealer
11 Warner Publicity Ltd., Advertising Contractors

11 Shaw, Christine, Co., Beauty Specialists
12 Ghana Airways Corporation
13 Benson & Hedges Ltd., Cigar Merchants
13 Leger Galleries Ltd., Fine Art Dealers
14 Colnaghi, P. & D., & Co., Ltd., Fine Art Dealers
15 RAYNE HOUSE:
FIRST FLOOR
Amcel Ltd., Man-made Fibre Manufacturers
THIRD FLOOR
Dorland & Partners, Consultant Surveyors
Townsend Thorensen Properties Ltd., Property Developers
Gadoil U.K. Ltd., Oil Brokers
FOURTH FLOOR
Rayne, H. & M., (Sales) Ltd., Footwear Manufacturers
MMG, Mario Maraldi Group, Pipe Fittings Manufacturers
Carratu, A. D. J., Accountant
16 Rayne, H. & M. Ltd., Shoe Retailers
16 Delman Ltd., Hand-made Shoes
16 Anglo-Irish Agency Ltd., Bloodstock Exporters
16 Max Factor, Hollywood & London (Sales) Ltd., Cosmetics (Offices)
17/18 Ward, Howell International Ltd., Business Consultants
17 & 18 Orlik, L., Ltd., Tobacco Pipe Manufacturers
17/18 Bennett, Toocaze Ltd., Fancy Leather Goods Manufacturers
17/18 Clough Antiques
17/18 Tallent, Roy, Ltd., Musical Boxes
17/18 Cyclax Ltd., Wholesale Toilet Preparations
17/18 Boggaert, André, Ltd., Retail Jewellers
17/18 Czechoslovak Travel Bureau (Cedok London Ltd.), Travel Agents
17/18 Czechoslovak Airlines

19 & 21 ROTHERWICK HOUSE:
Juschi Ltd., Leather Goods
Zapex (U.K.) Ltd., Oil Exploration
Zapata International Corporation, Oil Exploration
Air Holdings Ltd.
Airwork Services Ltd., Aeronautical Engineers

22 Clynold Ltd., Hairdressing School
22 Atcost Group, Prefabricated Building Manufacturers
22 Iran-Caspian Ltd., Export Agents
22 Torrini Ltd., Italian Jewellers
23 Truefitt & Hill (Old Bond Street) Ltd., Hairdressers
23 Humphris, Cyril, Fine Art Dealers
23 Roughton & Partners, Consulting Engineers
23 Cawston & Partners, Quantity Surveyors
23 Bahama Islands Tourist Office
23 Bahamas Ministry of Tourism
23 Burlington Health Club for Men, Physical Culture Institute
24 Kent, G. B., & Sons, Ltd., Brush Manufacturers
24 Cosby Brushes Ltd., Toilet Brush Makers
24 Titterton & Howard Ltd., Brush Makers
24 New, Court & Partners, Ltd., Management Consultants
24 Ferragamo Retail Ltd., Shoe Retailers
24 Oiltools International Ltd. (Oiltools Middle East Inc.), Oilfield Equipment Supplies and Service

Here are Burlington Gardens and New Bond Street

25 Mappin & Webb Ltd., Goldsmiths
25a Loewe, Leather Goods
26 Inghams Travel/Hotelplan, Travel Agents
26 Autoplan Travel Service Ltd.

27 ARCADE HOUSE:
   Gucci Ltd., Leather Goods
   Directors' Secretaries Ltd.
   Peerless Umbrellas Ltd., Umbrella Manufacturers
   Failsworth Hats (London) Ltd.
   Hoppen, Seymour Agencies Ltd., Men's Knitwear Manufacturers
   Spiller & Richards, Knitwear Agents
   White, Patrick, Architect
   Sogec, Commodity Brokers
   M. & A. International (Exclusive Agencies) Ltd., Manufacturers' Agents
   Politi, B., & Co., Ltd., Estate Agents
   Walters, Phyllis, Public Relations Consultant

Here is the Royal Arcade

28 Charbonnel & Walker Ltd., Chocolate Manufacturers
29 Holmes (Jewellers) Ltd.
29 Offenbach & Co., Solicitors
30 Bally London Shoe
30 Robinson, Gavin L. B., Ltd., Model Agency
30 Glaser, W. & A., Ltd., Jersey Wear Wholesalers
30 Sarony, Peter, & Associates, Architects
30 Lawson, Nicholas, Ltd., Overseas Hotels Representatives
30 Snell, John E., Estate Agent
30 Hunter, C., Ladies' Tailor
31 Susan Ltd., Shoes and Handbags
33 Yardley of London Ltd., Perfumery Makers
33 Germaine, Monteil (U.K.) Ltd., Cosmetic Manufacturers

Here is Stafford Street

35 Skinner & Co., Jewellers
35 Beautisales Ltd., Toilet Preparations
35 Yates, Gordon, Ltd., Secretarial Staff Consultancy
35 Marlborough Rare Books Ltd., Antiquarian Booksellers
35 Midland Bank Insurance Services Ltd.
35 Customline Ltd., Presentation Boxes
36 Midland Bank Ltd.
37 Soos, Andrew, Ltd., Leather Goods Retailers
38 Charig Ltd., Jewellers
38 Sharp, M. & S., Furriers
39 Lloyds Bank Ltd.
41 Brook Street Bureau of Mayfair Ltd., Employment Agency
43 Agnew, Thos., & Sons, Ltd., Dealers in Works of Art
44 Kirkby & Bunn, Ltd., Jewellers
45 Sac Frères, Amber Specialists
48 Ciro Pearls Ltd., Jewellers
49 Australian Tourist Commission
49 Qantas Airways Ltd.
49 American Airlines Inc., Air Line
49 Eastern Air Line Inc.

Here is Piccadilly

NEW BOND STREET

1 National Westminster Bank Ltd.
1 Viyash, Hunt & Co., Solicitors

1/5 NEW BOND STREET HOUSE:
  Siris (A. J.) Products Ltd., Toilet Requisites Manufacturers
  Yule, Catto & Co., Ltd., Holding Company
  Amari Ltd., Industrial Holding Company
  Amari World Steel Ltd., Stainless Steel Distributors
  Amari World Metals Ltd., Metal Merchants
  Aalco Ltd., Non-ferrous Metal Stockholders
  Town Centre Securities Ltd., Property Development Company
  Moret & Limberg, Accountants
  Booz, Allen & Hamilton International N.V., Management Consultants
  Pentos Holdings Ltd.
  Portuguese National Tourist Information Centre
4 Sabin, Frank T., Ltd., Printsellers
4 Green, Richard, Fine Art Dealer
5 Watches of Switzerland, Rolex Showroom, Watchmakers
6/7 Aigner, Etienne, Ltd., Leather Goods and Accessories
8 Godman & Rabey Ltd., Diamond Mounters
8 Mitchell, John, & Son, Picture Dealers
8 Jones & Burton Ltd., Diamond Setters
8 Trouser House, Men's Wear
9 Platinum Shop (The)
9/9a Booty Jewellery, Jewellery Retailers
9/9a Gibson, Thomas, Fine Art, Ltd., Fine Art Dealers
9/9a Telcom Personnel Recruitment, Employment Agents
9/9a West Danes, & Co., Personnel Consultants
10a Yeo, R. W., Ltd., Jewellers
10 Davis, Adèle, Ladies' Outfitter
10 Broomfield, John, & Co., Estate Agents
10 Togo Consulate
11 Antrobus, Philip, Ltd., Manufacturing and Retail Jewellers
12 Reger, Janet, Ltd., Couture, Lingerie

12 Publiter Ltd., Advertising Agents
13/14 Career Girl, Recruitment Consultancy
13/14 Multi Star Agency, Theatrical Agents
13 Oriental Carpet Galleries, Carpet Retailers
14 Town & Country Clothes Ltd., Knitwear
14a Plaget, Watch Retailers
15 Jensen, Georg, (Silversmiths), Ltd.
16 Watches of Switzerland Ltd.
Here is Clifford Street
17/18 Air India, Air Transport
18 Aerolineas Argentinas, Air Line
20 Arden, Elizabeth, Toilet Preparations
20 Wardrobe, Ladies' Outfitters
21 India (Government of), Tourist Office
22 Cameo Corner Ltd., Antique Jewellers
22 Fior Ltd., Costume Jewellery
23 Cuero, Leather Clothing Retailers
23 Landau, Philip, Men's Wear
  Westbury Hotel
Here is Conduit Street
24 & 25 Russell & Bromley Ltd., Boot and Shoe Retailers
24/25 M.A.M. Ltd., Theatrical Agents
26 Tessiers Ltd., Goldsmiths, Silversmiths and Jewellers
27 Interlingua Translation, Language Translators
27 Financial Associates (London) Ltd.
27 Castel, Fashion House
27 Chard of London Ltd., Shirt Manufacturers
27 Vanderkar, Dennis, Gallery, Fine Art Dealers
28 Celine-Paris, Leather Cloth Retailers
28 Louis, Ladies' Tailor
28 Feilding, Jocelyn, Picture Dealer
29 Christina, Ladies' Fashions
29 Elson of Sweden, Men's Wear Wholesalers
29 Elma Sportswear Ltd., Sports Goods Wholesalers
29 Overton, Mary, Employment Agency
30 Thorncroft, Michael, Chartered Surveyor
30 Sigma Resources Inc., Oil Exploration
30 Abbar & Zainy (London), Food Distributors
30 Corporate Direction Ltd., Management Consultants

67 Just Looking, Ladies' Fashions
67/68 Eden, E., Manufacturing Furrier
67/68 Bieber (Kenneth) Photography Ltd., Commercial Photographers
67/68 Cantor Art Service Ltd., Design Consultants
67/68 Cantor Jonathan Associates Ltd., Advertising Agents
67 Royal Society of Medicine (The), Photographic Unit
68 Susan of London, Ladies' Handbags
68 Myers Office Equipment Ltd., Office Furniture and Equipment
69 Coronel Ltd., Fashion Shops
69 Emka Productions Ltd., Artists' Management
70 Brasserie (The), Licensed Restaurant
70/71 Nu-Type Secretarial Bureau Ltd., Employment Agency
70/71 Murty, Anthony, & Co., Chartered Accountants
70/71 Joseph, E. P., Ltd., Stainless Steel Goods
70/71 Adpower Ltd., Staff Consultants
70/71 North Eastern Clothing Co., Ltd., Clothing Manufacturers
70/71 Heather Mills Co., Ltd., Scotch Tweed Manufacturers
71 Jones Menswear
72 U.S. News & World Report
72 Chemometal Products Ltd., Chemical Merchants
72 Midas, Shoe Retailers
72 Unisel Ltd., Export Merchants
72 Stillitron (Stillit Books Ltd.), Publishers
73 Albany Accountants Ltd., Employment Agency
73 Executive Secretarial Services Ltd., Employment Agency
73 Executive Secretaries Ltd., Employment Agency
73 Management Consultants (Selection) Ltd., Employment Agents
73 Saint Laurent (Rive Gauche), Fashion House
73 de Carle, John, & Associates, Contact Lens Practitioners
73 Baratte (Paul) International Ltd., Export Management and Marketing
73 Hackman & Co., Ltd., Export Merchants

73 Geraldo Orchestras Ltd.
74 Juran, Alexander, & Co., Carpet Importers
74 Yarden Ltd., Carpet Restorers
75 Lothars Ltd., Fashions
75 Miller, B., Turf Accountant
75 Workhouse (The), Employment Agency
75 Claton Consultants Ltd., Employment Agency

Here is Dering Street

76/78 Elliott, T., & Sons, Ltd., Shoe Retailers
77 Apollo Holidays Ltd., Tour Operators
77 London Office Facilities, Accommodation Address Service
77 Senior Staff Selection, Employment Agency
77 Renaissance Fine Arts Ltd., Printsellers
77 Socialist Commentary Publications Ltd.
78 Joseph & Wagg, Theatrical Agents
78 Ratcliffes, Property Consultants
79 Gibson, Ivy, Marriage Bureau
79 Melville, Stephen, & Co., Estate Agents
79 Francisco M., Menswear

80 RAVENSEFT HOUSE:
Ravenseft Properties Ltd.
Manfield & Sons, Ltd., Shoe Retailers
Sevington Properties Ltd.

Here is Oxford Street

87/89 Dolcis Ltd., Boot and Shoe Retailers
90 Take Six, Men's Wear
91 DOLCIS HOUSE:
87/91 Sant, Howard Partnership, Chartered Architects
87/91 Blackwood, Morton & Sons, Ltd., Carpet Manufacturers
87/91 Somers, Baker & Partners, Chartered Accountants
87/91 Levine, A. R., Andrews & Co., Chartered Accountants
87/91 International Labour Office, Publishers
87/91 Turin International Centre, Training Consultants
91 Triumph International Ltd., Corset Manufacturers
92 Elle, Fashions
93 Albany Artists Ltd., Commercial Artists
93 Bill, W., Ltd., Woollen Merchants

94 TARTAN HOUSE:
Astor Appointments, Employment Agency

Old Vienna Restaurant
Stirling, Ronnie, Boutique

Here is Blenheim Street

95 Fios Slumberland Ltd., Continental Quilts
95 Geiger, Kurt, Shoe Retailers
95 Place Vendôme, Fashions
96 Maynard, Robert, Ltd., Knitwear Merchants
96 Heath, Peter, & Partners, Consulting Engineers
97 Royal Bank of Scotland
96 Garrod, Smedey & Co., Surveyors
97 Royal Philharmonic Orchestra Ltd.
98 B.U.K. Records Ltd., Record Producers
98 Frette, Linen Specialists
99 Bond Street Boutique Ltd., Knitwear Dealers
99 Deimel House, Underwear Retailers
99 Brainin Bros., Manufacturing Furriers
100 Zakhem Construction Services Ltd., Constructional Engineers
100 Collyer Daish Associates, Advertising Agents
100 Pick, R. A., & Co., Chartered Accountants
100 Robson, Lawrie & Co., Chartered Accountants
100 Skincraft (U.K.) Ltd., Suede Clothing Retailers
101 Warren, Diana, Fashions
101 Davis, Henry, & Co., Chartered Surveyors
102 Crocodile, Ladies' Fashions
103 Ravel, Ladies' Shoe Retailers

104 Milbanke house:
T.H.F. Travel, Travel Agents
Fourways Travel Ltd., Continental Tour Operators

105 Hechter, Daniel, Boutique, Men's, Women's and Children's Wear
105/106 Croft Maxwell Ltd., Manufacturing Furriers
105 & 106 Gross & Fuss Ltd., Fashion Agents
106/106 Dennis & Alan, Manufacturing Furriers
105/106 Caplin, Chas., & Co., Solicitors
106 Ryman Ltd., Office Furnishers
107 British Airways
107 Greenwood, T., Furs, Manufacturing Furriers

107 Irving Furs, Manufacturing Furriers
107 Margaritta, Milliner
108 Boselli, E., & Co., Ltd., Textile Manufacturers
108 Young, Raymond, Beauty Therapist
108 St. Paul's Employment Agency Ltd.
108 Chavila (Bond St.) Ltd., Men's Wear
109 Way, Stephen, Ltd., Ladies' Hairdressers
109 Clifford, Max, Associates, Public Relations Consultants
110 Le Soir Handbags Ltd.
110 Drown, William (Bond Street) Ltd., Picture Restorers
110 Russell & Bromley Ltd., Shoe Retailers
110 Matisse Blouses Ltd., Blouse Manufacturers
110 Tollemache, Michael, Ltd., Picture Dealers
110a Wolmark, David, Ltd., Watchmakers
110a Wolmark, P. Howard, Dispensing Optician

Here is Brook Street

111/112 Bond Street Silver Galleries Ltd.
111/112 Angel & Kaye, Antique Silver and Plate Dealers
111/112 Black, Arthur, Antique Silver and Plate Dealer
111/112 Black, Henry (Antiques) Ltd., Antique Silver and Plate Dealers
111/112 Bloomstein, A. & B., Ltd., Antique Silver and Plate Dealers
111/112 Fortunoff (U.S.A.), Antique Silver and Plate Dealers
111/112 Frydman, Oszer, Antique Silver and Plate Dealers
111/112 Glass, G., & Son, Antique Silver and Plate Dealers
111/112 Bull, John, Ltd., Antique Silver and Plate Dealers
111/112 Swonnell, E. G. (Silverware) Ltd., Antique Silver and Plate Dealers
113 Saint Laurent (Rive Gauche), Fashion House
114 Magli, Shoe Retailers
114 Intereurope Communications Ltd., Public Relations Consultants
114 Kneller, Davis & Co., Accountants
114 Creative Talent Associates Ltd., Music Publishers
114 Chappell, Aznavour Ltd., Music Publishers

163

The publishers of this book acknowledge with appreciation the kindness of Kelly's Directories Ltd. in allowing reproduction of the above lists, extracted from various editions of *Kelly's Post Office London Directory*. The 1978 list, however, has been updated by Pauline Tooth of the Bond Street Association.

BOND STREET
ANNOUNCEMENTS

It takes more than a fashionable address

33 OLD BOND STREET

to keep a reputation fashionable

We have come a long way since Yardley, Bond Street and the Lavender Lady came to fame. Our products are to be found in over 142 countries with 38 factories supplying over 2,000 different products that make women beautiful and desirable the world over.

Yardley and Bond Street stand famously together; as they have done since 1770 – and never more up-to-date than today!

yardley

London's Traditional Treasure House

Asprey

Asprey and Company Limited, 165-169 New Bond Street, London W1Y 0AR. Telephone: 01-493 6767.

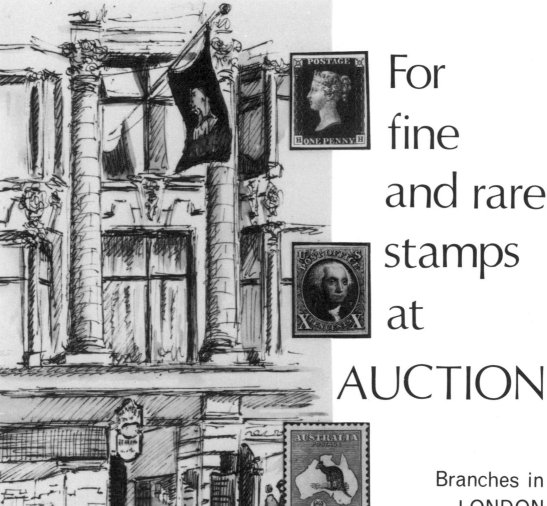

CHANEL

Paul Salgo Paul Salgo

Silk Silk Silk Silk Sil

Paul Salgo Paul Salgo

Silk Silk Silk Silk Sil

Paul Salgo Paul Salgo

Silk Silk Silk Silk Sil

Paul Salgo Paul Salgo

**Bond Street's producers of hand-made silk ties and dressing gowns.
At Number 39. Telephone: 01-629 2992.**

Paul Salgo Paul Salgo

Silk Silk Silk Silk Sil

A picture that is a symbol: the statue of Justice overlooking the Feroni-Spini Palace, a jewel of thirteenth century Florence, birthplace of the prestigious SALVATORE FERRAGAMO. Ferragamo and Florence: a natural union between a city of Art and a family that has made Art its own vocation, creating first shoes, then ready to wear for men and women.

Salvatore Ferragamo
Firenze

FERRAGAMO 24 OLD BOND ST. LONDON W1· 01 629 5007

It was over one hundred and sixty five years ago that Samuel Chappell founded his music business and quickly established an impressive reputation as a music publisher, seller of quality pianos and promoter of fine performances.

For almost a century, Chappell and Co. remained essentially a family business until the death, in 1902, of Samuel's son, Thomas.

During this time, having moved the company to its present address in New Bond Street, Thomas did much to promote music and its appeal. In the 1850's he helped finance and build St. James's Hall, Piccadilly and initiated the popular concerts that have now become the "Proms."

In the 1860's he engaged Charles Dickens to give readings from his popular novels and purchased the publishing rights to such diverse works as Balfe's "Bohemian Girl," Gounod's "Faust" and the first of Gilbert and Sullivan's light operas "Trial by Jury," – most of the rest were bought later.

But apart from publishing and printing the works of the best music writers, a tradition that continues today, Chappell and Co. became renowned as manufacturers of fine pianos. Indeed, the excellence of their craft was such that Richard Strauss paid tribute to a Chappell piano made specially for him and later the famous pianist Wilhelm Backhaus wrote:

"I feel it both a duty and a pleasure to thank you for your two magnificent Concert Grand Pianofortes used by me during my first tour in Great Britain.

I cannot speak too highly of the brilliant and sympathetic tone and responsive touch possessed by them. I can confidently say you need fear no rival."

Today the Chappell Music Centre in Bond Street is one of the most up to date and comprehensive in Europe and can offer its customers an unrivalled selection of musical goods to choose from; records and tapes, audio equipment, sheet music and song books, theatre and concert tickets, musical instruments, organs and, of course, pianos.

Chappell & Co. Ltd., 50 New Bond Street, London W1.

Since their establishment in the late eighteenth century, Savory & Moore have had the honour of serving some of the most distinguished people in English Society.

Today the shop's exterior has a quaint old world charm but, once inside, you will find a range of the most modern and, in many cases, the most exclusive products available in London.

SAVORY & MOORE

143, New Bond Street,
London W.1.
Tel: 01 629 4471

REGRETTABLY, NOT EVERYONE IN LONDON IS ABLE TO BANK WITH US.

Drummonds Branch
49 Charing Cross LONDON SW1A 2DX Tel No. 01-930 1711/7
01-930 4768/9 Manager: Mr J H Shaw

Regent Street Branch
Vigo House 115 Regent Street
LONDON W1A 3DD
Tel No. 01-439 6091 01-734 5491
Manager: Mr G Macdonald

Mayfair Branch
5 Curzon Street LONDON W1Y 8BU Tel No. 01-499 4476
01-409 0229 Manager: Mr R W Bruce

Victoria Branch
120 Victoria Street LONDON SW1E 5LA
Tel No. 01-834 6302/3 Manager: Mr I Findlay

Piccadilly Circus Branch
48 Haymarket LONDON SW1Y 4SE
Tel No. 01-930 1396
Manager: Mr A E Drysdale

Bond Street Branch
97 New Bond Street
LONDON W1Y 0EU
Tel No. 01-629 2157/8
and 01-629 0030
Manager: Mr T H Farmer

Western Branch Burlington Gardens LONDON W1X 2AT Tel No. 01-734 4881
Manager: Mr W Bruce

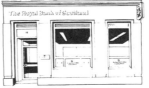

Kingsway Branch Imperial House 15 Kingsway
LONDON WC2B 6UR Tel No. 01-836 5896
Manager: Mr J Brown

Bishopsgate Office 3 Bishopsgate
LONDON EC2N 3AA Tel No. 01-283 2991
Manager: Mr A McIlwraith

Knightsbridge Branch 44 Brompton Road LONDON SW3 1BN
Tel No. 01-584 8492/3 Manager: Mr A Matthew

The London offices of The Royal Bank of Scotland remain somewhat exclusive.

There are still only eleven. In terms of numbers, not a great deal. In terms of service, however, still offering those exceptionally high standards our personal and corporate customers have rightly come to expect from the number one bank in Scotland.

Where we are less exclusive, with almost 600 Branches.

The Royal Bank of Scotland
You'll get on better with us.

Lombard Street Office P O Box 412 62 Lombard Street
LONDON EC3P 3DE Tel No. 01-623 1931 and 8321
Manager: Mr A B Murray

General Manager (London)—Mr John M Mowat, Bishopsgate Office,
3 Bishopsgate, London EC2N 3AA. Tel No. 01-283 2991.
The Royal Bank of Scotland Limited. Registered Office: 42 St. Andrew Square, Edinburgh EH2 2YE. Registered in Scotland Number 46419.

FAR-AWAY PLACES
APARTMENTS & PACKAGE TOURS
SELF-CATERING HOLIDAYS
SUMMER SUN
WINTER SPORTS
FLIGHT RESERVATIONS
AIR TICKETS
BRITISH RAIL TICKETS
CONTINENTAL RAIL TICKETS
SLEEPERS & COUCHETTES
CAR FERRIES
SEA PASSAGES & CRUISES
LUXURY COACH TOURS OF EUROPE
ARCHAEOLOGICAL TOURS
ART TREASURE TOURS
GROUP HOLIDAY BOOKINGS
BUSINESS TRAVEL
CONFERENCES & EXHIBITIONS
TRAVEL INCENTIVES
TRAVELSPORTS
CAR HIRE
HOTEL RESERVATIONS
SIGHT-SEEING & EXCURSIONS
THEATRE TICKETS
TRAVEL INSURANCE

**TRUST
HOUSES
FORTE
TRAVEL
LIMITED**

INCORPORATING MILBANKE TRAVEL, FLAIR, FLAIRWORLD, FOURWAYS, W. F. & R. K. SWAN (HELLENIC)
HEAD OFFICE: 104 NEW BOND STREET, LONDON, W1Y 0AE.
TELEPHONE: 01-493 8494

MALLETT

MALLETT & SON (ANTIQUES) LTD   40 NEW BOND STREET   LONDON W1Y OBS
TELEPHONE 01-499 7411   TELEX 25692

and at:
BOURDON HOUSE, 2 DAVIES STREET
BERKELEY SQUARE, LONDON, W1Y 1LJ

An extremely fine Charles II lacquer cabinet with original
carved giltwood cresting and stand, flanked by two magnificent
silver gilt pilgrim bottles, above a pair of Queen Anne black
and gold lacquer side chairs.

SPECIALISTS IN THE FINEST ENGLISH AND
CONTINENTAL ANTIQUE FURNITURE, CLOCKS,
OBJETS D'ART AND DECORATIVE PICTURES.

As right as Rayne...

RAYNE
Shoemakers

15-16 Old Bond Street London W1

WALLACE HEATON
FOUNDED 1839

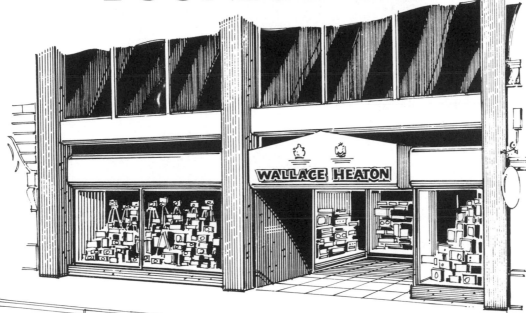

For such a young outfit, we offer a very old-fashioned service.

As you'd expect, the home of London's finest camera shop is in Bond Street.

That shop is Wallace Heaton – famous the world over for all that's best in Photography, Audio, Binoculars, Video and Calculators.

Bond Street has been in existence since 1686. Wallace Heaton was established in

1839. Relative newcomers, we agree.

However, we've been around long enough to remember the days when service was service. When shops were staffed by experts who delighted in helping the customer to make exactly the right choice.

If you want to be reminded of that kind of service, call into Wallace Heaton today.

BY APPOINTMENT TO
HER MAJESTY THE QUEEN
SUPPLIERS OF
PHOTOGRAPHIC EQUIPMENT
WALLACE HEATON LTD, LONDON

BY APPOINTMENT TO
HRH THE DUKE OF EDINBURGH
SUPPLIERS OF
PHOTOGRAPHIC EQUIPMENT
WALLACE HEATON LTD, LONDON

WALLACE HEATON
127, New Bond Street, W.1. Telephone 629 7511
And Branches at ◇ 1 Leadenhall Street, EC3 ◇ 63 Cheapside, EC2 ◇ 47 Berkeley Street, W1 ◇ Bentalls of Kingston-upon-Thames
By post: pay full price by cheque, Access or Barclaycard, quoting number.

International clothes for the International Woman

174 NEW BOND STREET · LONDON W1Y 9PB
TELEPHONE: 01-499 7733